SELF-PUBLISHING BOOT CAMP GUIDE FOR AUTHORS

3rd Edition

Carla King

Misadventures Media

San Diego, California

Copyright © 2015 by Carla King
Release 1/29/2015 : Update 7/16/2015

All rights reserved. No part of this publication may be reproduced, distributed or transmitted in any form or by any means, without prior written permission.

Carla King
Misadventures Media
2907 Shelter Island Drive
San Diego, CA 92106
www.selfpubbootcamp.com

Self-Publishing Boot Camp Guide for Authors -- 3rd ed. Print.
ISBN 978-0-9646445-9-5

For a typical author, obscurity is a far greater threat than piracy.

—TIM O'REILLY

I will not be "famous," "great." I will go on adventuring, changing, opening my mind and my eyes, refusing to be stamped and stereotyped. The thing is to free one's self: to let it find its dimensions, not be impeded.

—VIRGINIA WOOLF

Update Notes

Thank you for your continued review and input on the development of this ever-updated series. An honest review on Amazon is much appreciated. I strive to make each edition better than the last. You can contribute a book review by finding this 3rd edition on my author page. Type in "Carla King Amazon Author Page" in your search engine. Or find it by following this URL: http://www.amazon.com/Carla-King/e/B004FWBLQ6

February 1, 2015
Released BETA book exclusively as a giveaway for BookBaby.

April 2, 2015
Incorporated input from BETA book and published ebook and print versions for sale to online retailers and brick-and-mortar bookstores.

July 17, 2015
1. Removed Vook as a trusted vendor. Vook has changed its business model many times over the years and often for the better. Self-publishing has been a rapidly developing industry and I don't discount them for that. In mid-2015 they changed their name to Pronoun and though their new model looks quite attractive they have not really started serving authors yet. If you have published with Vook rest assured that they continue honor their previous distribution agreements.
2. Changed right-side headers to match the chapter heads for easier navigation through the book as suggested by readers.
3. Replaced some images with sharper versions. Please note that screen shots are inherently of poor quality, and I've attempted to make them as sharp as possible.
4. Defined "gravatar" on first use on the suggestion of a reader.

CONTENTS

MY PUBLISHING ADVENTURE	ix
HOW THIS BOOK IS ORGANIZED	xiii
YOUR AUTHOR TOOLSET	1
Microsoft Word and alternatives	2
Word styles and templates	3
Word alternatives	4
PressBooks	6
Scrivener	8
Adobe InDesign	10
Leanpub	11
Draft	12
Others worth noting	14
Your favorites?	15
YOUR PUBLISHING PATH	**17**
Retailer-specific tools	19
Creating your ebook	20
Distributing your ebook	20

Creating your print book	21
Distributing your print book	22
Services that distribute both print and ebooks	22
Reader subscription programs	23
Independent book formatting services	23
Hybrid publishing	25
Traditional distribution	27
Book packagers	29
Book producers	30
Printing companies	31
Literary agents	31
Vanity presses	32
TRUSTED VENDORS	**35**
Aerbook and Aer.io	37
Amazon CreateSpace	38
Amazon Kindle Direct Publishing (KDP)	39
Amazon Kindle Kids' Book Creator	41
Blurb	41
Book Design Templates	42
BookBaby	43
Bowker	45
GoDaddy	46
Gumroad	46
IngramSpark	47
Leanpub	50
Lightning Source	51
MailChimp	51

PressBooks	51
Scribd	53
Scrivener	53
Slicebooks	54
Smashwords	54
WordPress	58
Your trusted tools and services?	58
YOUR PUBLISHING BUSINESS	**61**
Publisher name	62
Fictitious business name	62
Other financial and legal concerns	63
Your budget	64
The real cost to publish your book	65
Developing a business plan	68
Your mission and goals	68
Raising funds	70
Author Crowdfunding	71
Publisher-Assisted Crowdfunding	74
Your sales strategy	75
Pricing your book	78
Setting expectations	79
The Bowker record and ISBNs	79
Registering your copyright	82
Getting into libraries	84
Library of Congress CIP number	86
Library of Congress PCN program	86
Local Libraries	87
Copyright	88
Ebooks to Libraries	88

Smashwords and Overdrive	88
Using the same distributor as for print	89
SELF-e	90

YOUR AUTHOR BRAND — 93

Understanding brand	93
Elements of your brand	98
Your author bio	99
Your author photo	101

WEBSITES & BLOGS — 105

Choosing a domain name	106
Choosing web hosting	108
Building your website	112
Setting up your blog	115
Widgets and social media links	117
Twitter	117
Facebook	118
WordPress Widgets for Flicker, Goodreads, etc.	118
Document Sharing Widgets	119
YouTube	119

MARKETING & PROMOTION — 121

Your mailing list	122
Hiring out publicity	125
Your online press kit	127
Press releases	127
Book reviews	128
Professional organizations	132
Trade organizations	133
Make your book discoverable	134

Amazon's promotional tools	134
Amazon Author Central	135
Kindle KDP Select	136
Amazon Customer Reviews	138
Goodreads	138
Amazon Associates	138
So You'd Like to . . . guides	139
Look Inside the Book	139
SOCIAL MEDIA MARKETING	**141**
Grab your name	142
Twitter	143
Twitter apps	143
Hashtags	143
Facebook	144
Google+	145
Images in social media	146
LinkedIn	146
YouTube	147
Social publishing	147
Forums and groups	148
The social media rule of thirds	148
Connecting with readers in the social stream	149
Streamline your social media tasks	150
Widgets encourage sharing	152
EDITING & PROOFREADING	**155**
Book consultants	159
Writing groups	159
Calculate time to completion	162
Professional editing and proofreading	163

Printing proofs	165
BOOK DESIGN	**167**
Research books in your genre	170
Standard book sizes	172
Interior typography, fonts, and dingbats	173
Paper stock	173
Spine width	174
Detailed book specification	175
Print book covers	176
Ebook covers	177
Book design services	178
The importance of styles	179
Design templates	180
Hiring a professional	180
Creating print ready files	181
METADATA & DISCOVERY	**183**
Your keywords list	185
Title and description tags	187
Metadata for images	188
Your Bowker record	188
What is an ISBN and do you really need one?	191
Buying and managing ISBNs	192
What formats need separate ISBNs?	194
The Books In Print database	197
Barcodes	197
Metadata in documents and other media	198
Metadata on reseller sites	200
Metadata on social media sites	201

Creating a gravatar ... 201
EBOOKS ... 203
Ebook formatting and conversion basics ... 205
Ebook formats ... 207
    EPUB ... 208
    Kindle ... 209
    PDF ... 210
Ebook readers ... 211
Do-it-for-you services ... 213
Doing it yourself ... 214
Creating complex ebooks ... 217
Social publishing ... 219
Ebook aggregation ... 221
    Sales and distribution channels ... 222
Scanning your print book ... 224
Setting the begin reading point ... 225
DRM and copyright protection ... 226
Your digital publishing path ... 227
PRINT BOOKS ... 229
Print your proof ... 231
Advance reading copies (ARCs) ... 231
Print-on-demand (POD) ... 234
Short run printing ... 234
Offset printing ... 235
    Compose a Request for Quote (RFQ) ... 237
    Hire a print broker ... 238
Full service vendors ... 238
Barcodes ... 239

RESOURCES	**241**
ABOUT THE AUTHOR	**245**
ACKNOWLEDGEMENTS	**247**
EVENTS, WORKSHOPS & CONFERENCES	**249**
WHAT NEXT?	**251**

PREFACE

MY PUBLISHING ADVENTURE

I love travel. I love writing. And I love the control that self-publishing gives me. I self-published my first book, a little guide to bicycling around Nice in the south of France titled *Cycling the French Riviera,* in 1994. I'd lived there for six months and wrote it because there was no guide, not even in French.

I'd worked as a tech writer for a few years by then, and I knew how to write instruction manuals, so it was actually pretty easy. When I came home, I shopped my book around to agents and publishers, and they all said it was good, but it was too small. They'd consider it if I went back to cover the rest of the region, all the way from the Italian border west to Marseille.

But I wasn't going to do that. And I was sure that there was an audience for my book. So I got my geeky self down to publishing it on my own. Production wasn't that difficult considering that I'd already written and published a huge stack of technical manuals. But getting a cover design, an ISBN and distribution was all new.

In the end, I printed 500 books, flew back to France and hand-sold them from the trunk of a rented car to tourist offices, bicycle shops, and English-language bookstores. I ended up with about $1000 profit, and that was *after* expenses, and thus began my love affair with self-publishing.

Since then I have produced and published many other books, on my own and with partners and a whole lot of online books and magazines. Many of my stories are also published in anthologies.

In about 2008 other writers, even traditionally published authors, started asking me how to self-publish, so I wrote the first version of this how-to guide and started teaching classes. Since then, Self-Pub Boot Camp sure has grown up! Now it's an entire program of books, seminars, and virtual workshops.

PREFACE

Today self-publishing is mainstream, but authors are still confused about the process. It really is a different language, a different country with unfamiliar customs. I love exploring new languages, new countries and customs, and I also love technology. So I found a new passion guiding authors in their journeys to the right tools and services, to map this exciting new world.

As I said, I love travel, technology, writing, and publishing. So thank you for reading this book and allowing me be your guide to mapping out your self-publishing adventure.

How's your journey going? Please report back via the contact form on the SelfPubBootCamp.com site. ♥

HOW THIS BOOK IS ORGANIZED

This guide steps you through all the tasks required to create the ebook and print book of your dreams, whether you want to publish a simple text-heavy book, a lush, full-color book or a multimedia extravaganza for the new tablet readers. It provides recommendations for reputable tools and services and resources for getting reliable help completing tasks like editing, design, formatting and distribution. The information is arranged in roughly the order you need to address each step in your self-publishing path. Enjoy the journey!

1. Your author toolset

Find out about the tools that will help you create and publish your books. Learn about styles and formats in word processing and page layout programs, templates, and cloud-based services that export to both print and ebook formats.

2. Your publishing path

Identify your publishing choices and apply one or a combination of tools and services to your particular publishing scenario.

3. Vendors I trust

These are the vendors I trust most to assist you reliably in your independent publishing journey. (Find updates in my email newsletter at selfpubbootcamp.com.)

4. Your publishing business

Are you aiming for an international bestseller or will your book support your business, leave a legacy or fill a gap in a niche market? Start your business as a publisher, create a realistic budget, obtain a DBA, ISBNs, and copyright protection.

5. Your author brand

Create a recognizable brand using colors, logos, typography, photography, and a keyword-rich author bio. Consistently apply these elements to your website and social media properties, and in your book description and promotional materials.

6. Your website and weblog

Create a website and weblog that reflects your brand that centralizes your activities for your readers and the media. Buy domain names, choose a web hosting service, and start blogging.

7. Marketing and promotion

Get yourself noticed on the web, in print and among your peers. Find out how to build a mailing list, create a press kit, and use online services to connect with readers in social streams.

8. Your social media presence

Choose the social media sites best suited to your market. You don't have to use all of them, but you might as well sign up, grab your name, and create keyword-rich profiles that link to your website.

9. Editing and proofreading

Editing is one area where self-publishers often fail. Learn how to improve your writing by sharing with beta readers and writing groups. Get the most for your money with professional developmental editors, copyeditors, and proofreaders.

10. Designing your book's interior and cover

Hire a pro to make effective use of graphics, photography and typography to result in an attention-grabbing book cover. Start with a selection of beautiful, affordable, and time-saving book templates.

11. Metadata and discoverability

Metadata is your best passive marketing partner! Use SEO techniques and metadata so that your book ranks higher in search results. This topic is a little geeky but easier than you might think.

12. Ebook formatting and distribution

Learn about EPUB and MOBI for Kindle formats and, for complex books, fixed-layout formats for the new tablet devices. Distribute your book to all the ebook retailers using one or a combination of services.

13. Print book creation and distribution

Print proofs and advance reader copies of your book quickly and affordably. Learn about Print On Demand (POD), short run and offset printing and print brokers. Find out how to distribute books to the online retailers and brick-and-mortar bookstores.

Resources

Find the most current information on the self-publishing resources, along with the latest tools, technologies, products and services in this helpful list. ♥

CHAPTER ONE

YOUR AUTHOR TOOLSET

I begin this 3rd edition of *The Self-Publishing Boot Camp Guide for Authors* with a review of the author's toolset. Many free and low-cost tools have been developed just for us in the past few years. Yes, self-publishing is hot, and the indie author is a coveted customer. It's great to be able to choose from so many tools that ease the process of organizing, writing, editing, designing, and formatting books.

Even the tool we're most familiar with, Microsoft Word, has improved its feature set. Enterprising publishing pros have created book design templates based on Word that anyone can use. This alone saves us lots of time and money so we can concentrate on writing and marketing our books.

Of course, not every tool is for every author. And not every author uses their toolset to capacity. I hope that this chapter gives you the information you need to choose and use a toolset that will help you succeed in your indie publishing journey.

Now, let's explore the possibilities for your author toolbox.

- Microsoft Word and alternatives
- PressBooks
- Scrivener
- Adobe InDesign
- Draft
- Others worth noting
- Your favorites?

Microsoft Word and alternatives

Most authors use Word simply as a better typewriter, but this popular desktop application has evolved into a fully functional word processing and page layout program. It offers many features to help format documents and books, not the least of which are preconfigured "styles," which automate character, section, and paragraph formatting. When you work in Word to format your book, it's essential that you use styles instead of line and paragraph breaks, spaces and tabs. It's easy to learn to use Word styles, and I guarantee you'll save a lot of time, energy, and money formatting your books. Find out more on Microsoft's page on Style Basics in Word.

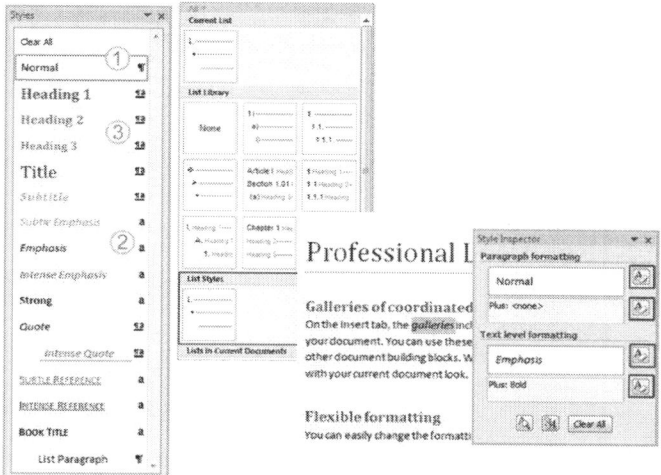

Using Microsoft Word styles saves a lot of time formatting your book.

You and your editors may already work together using Word's Track Changes feature. Alternate editing options I like are Google Drive, Draft, and Poetica, which also track changes. With these tools (described later in this chapter), your document lives in the cloud and not on the desktop, so everyone works on the same document, sometimes at the same time.

Word styles and templates

Now, how do you convert that Word document into a book? One of my favorite templates for making books is

Joel Friedlander's book design templates. (The other is PressBooks, described later in this chapter.) Joel offers templates both in Word and InDesign, and they're very affordable. You simply choose a design you like, paste your Word document into it, and apply the appropriate style to the title, subtitles, body text, and other elements (bulleted and numbered lists, pull quotes and such). If you like, you can modify the styles to get exactly the look you want. Joel provides easy instructions on how to use them.

The Book Designer Joel Friedlander has created low-cost book templates in Word and InDesign that make your book look beautiful and professional.

Word alternatives

I stopped using Word a long time ago, experimenting with a variety of alternatives on my Mac including Apple Pages, OpenOffice, and NeoOffice. They all offer the same set of features you see in Word, and they're compatible with Word documents.

The OpenOffice suite is a free and open source alternative to Microsoft Word. NeoOffice is a separate, optimized version of OpenOffice for the Mac operating system. LibreOffice is based on the OpenOffice project. I haven't used it (yet) but it seems interesting as they offer an extension that creates ebooks and educational materials. It's called eLAIX, and it converts LibreOffice Writer documents into ILIAS learning modules and EPUB ebooks. (If you know anything about it I would love to hear about your experience.)

All these office suites offer analogs to the Word suite of document creation programs. For example, Writer in place of Word, Calc instead of Excel, Impress for PowerPoint, and others.

 Writer a word processor you can use for anything from writing a quick letter to producing an entire book.

 Calc a powerful spreadsheet with all the tools you need to calculate, analyze, and present your data in numerical reports or sizzling graphics.

 Impress the fastest, most powerful way to create effective multimedia presentations.

 Draw lets you produce everything from simple diagrams to dynamic 3D illustrations.

 Base lets you manipulate databases seamlessly. Create and modify tables, forms, queries, and reports, all from within Apache OpenOffice.

 Math lets you create mathematical equations with a graphic user interface or by directly typing your formulas into the equation editor.

The OpenOffice Suite of tools is compatible with and competes with Microsoft Office.

If you compose your manuscript in any of these Word alternatives, don't worry, you can export it to Word to hand off to your editor for redlining. But you might suggest that they download it free, there's very little learning curve.

My nieces and nephews use OpenOffice and NeoOffice and, as the designated editor for their college essays, I have found that Track Changes works flawlessly among them. Paragraph and character styles also remain consistent when converting among Word and these alternatives. If you're on a budget or using an outdated or bootlegged version of Word, you may be attracted to using these tools instead of expensive Microsoft software.

PressBooks

PressBooks is an online publishing tool that produces beautifully-designed PDFs for print and print-on-demand. Use it to create print books that you publish using vendors like CreateSpace and IngramSpark, along with ebooks you publish on Kindle for Amazon and EPUB for Apple iBooks, Nook, and Kobo. It's built on the open source WordPress blogging platform so, if you're blogging on WordPress, you already know how to use it. I've created several books and booklets with PressBooks, including this one.

I like the PressBooks blog-to-book import feature, which is awesome for creating a first draft of a book from a series of blog posts. (Nina Amir is the guru on how to blog a book, and I also highly recommend her course on how to Write a Short Book Fast.)

Simply paste in text to the PressBooks interface on the web, and then choose one of their beautifully designed interior book themes. When you're you're ready, export your book to PDF, EPUB, and MOBI. It's free to play and to remove the watermark costs $25 for ebooks and $100 for ebook and print.

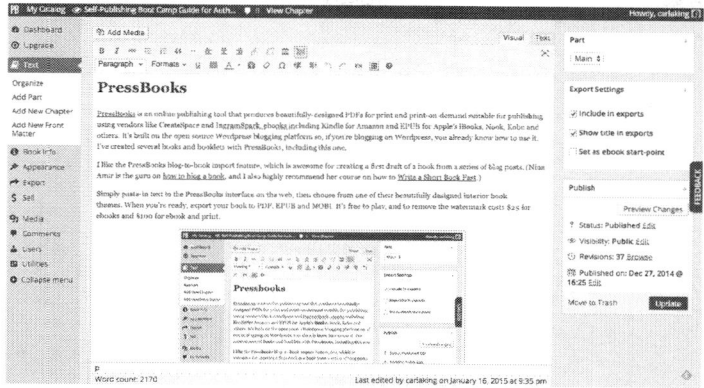

PressBooks is based on WordPress and uses CSS to style your book.

If you're intimidated by PressBooks, start small by using it to create a short book to give away to your email newsletter subscribers. Or pay PressBooks to do it all for you.

Just a few of PressBooks' many interior book themes.

Scrivener

Scrivener is a desktop writing and organization tool with an amazing feature set that can help you develop stories and books. Last year I started using it to organize and write my blog posts, articles, and books.

Scrivener also exports (they call it "compile") your book to just about any format you want, including PDF, Word and OpenOffice, EPUB, MOBI, HTML, and markdown languages.

Compile to doc format for Word if you're handing your book off to an editor who uses Word's Track Changes, or if you've decided to use one of Joel Friedlander's book design templates.

Scrivener is definitely worth the $45 (free 30-day trial) and the learning curve. There is a free series of YouTube videos but also a good manual and lots of paid training available. It took me about four hours to learn how to use all the features and was well worth the time invested.

Scrivener organizes material in "binders" that hold multiple documents, and it also offers an awesome bulletin board view. A scriptwriter friend started using the program years ago to replace the actual corkboard on his office wall, where he used to tack up cards with titles and sketches outlining his scripts. I love it because it replaces the need for nested folders and file trees on my hard drive. Now I gather research material in the same binder I create for a book, article or series of blog posts. In this way, Scrivener functions as a combination of the Evernote idea-saver and reminder program (your electronic brain) and word processing software. You can buy Scrivener for Windows or Mac.

I like Scrivener for organizing my writing and research as well as for exporting ebook and print book formats directly from the program.

Adobe InDesign

I still use Adobe InDesign because my older books were designed in it and occasionally I have to make corrections or updates. InDesign is book design software and the de-facto standard used by professional book designers. It's expensive and difficult to learn but extremely flexible, giving the designer ultimate control over ebook and print book design.

Self-publishers like me had to learn InDesign before all the easy-to-use solutions were developed. InDesign is part of the Adobe Creative Suite, which also includes PhotoShop, Illustrator, and other applications pro designers are trained to use. (Instead, you might use PhotoShop Elements or the free, open source GIMP program for manipulating images.)

If you have a serious budget for your book and want a real pro to design it for you, make sure the designer uses the latest version of InDesign.

As I mentioned above, Joel Friedlander offers book design templates in InDesign as well as Word templates, so you might want to use it to create a draft of your InDesign book. If you get stuck, you can always pay a professional to finish it.

Whenever I mention InDesign I have to mention Blurb, which offers an awesome tool called BookWright that's easy to use, but proprietary. (That means your book is not portable among book creation and distribution services.) Blurb also provides a plugin for InDesign. If you have an arty book with complex formatting you'll definitely want to check them out.

An alternative to doing it yourself is BookBaby, who can create your complex print book and fixed-layout ebook in InDesign, and distribute it to resellers, for a very reasonable fee. Leanpub also lets you export to InDesign, so when your beta test or crowdfunding campaign is done you can finesse your book with sophisticated formatting in InDesign.

Leanpub

Leanpub is an awesome online publishing system that was built for books in process, iterative books, and serials, so that your readers can buy the book before it's complete. This is great for nonfiction books that contains information that your readers might need right now, or for serials like travelogues—you can notify them that an update is ready. In this way it can be used as a paid blogging platform or for crowdfunding. Leanpub uses MarkDown language but exports to a lot of different formats.

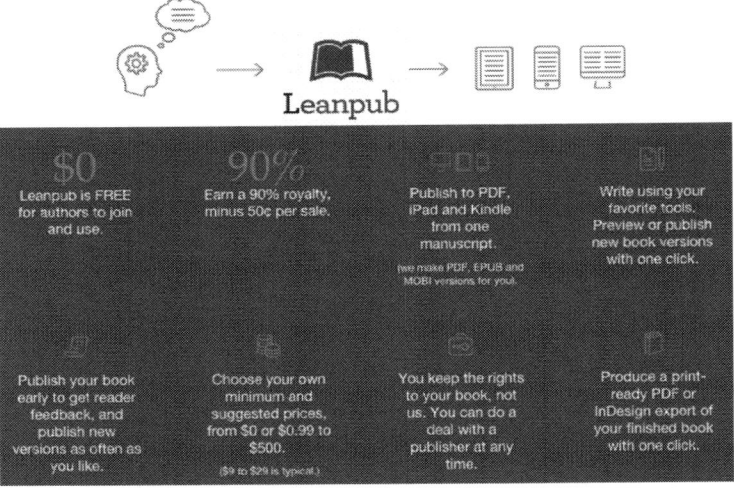

Leanpub is a publishing platform that exports to ebook and print formats, but it can also be used as a paid blogging platform or for crowdfunding.

Draft

Draft is a writing, editing, collaboration, and publishing tool in the cloud. Each contributor's changes show up in different colors, with accept and reject options. You can mark major revisions, find and revert to previous versions, import docs from Dropbox, Evernote and Google Drive, and publish directly to places like WordPress, Tumblr, LinkedIn, and even MailChimp. They've provided a handy Chrome extension that lets you turn any text area on the web into something you can write and edit with Draft.

You can email a document to your Draft account using a secret address, create a simple presentation, comment out segments of writing, and the "simplify" robot catches common words, duplicate words, and attempts to detect and delete unimportant sentences. More features include an audio-video transcription tool, analytics, and website builder tool. Hemingway mode provides distraction-free writing.

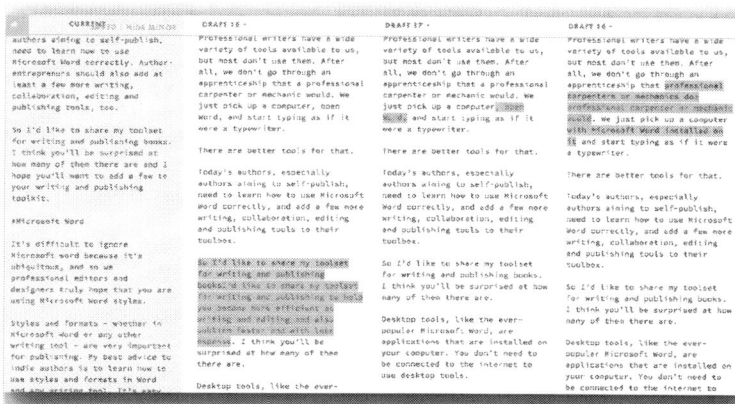

Draft makes it clear what changes have been made and lets you collaborate with many others in the cloud.

Others worth noting

There are many more writing, editing and publishing tools you might add to your writers' toolbox. For example, there's another great editing program called Poetica that uses traditional editing symbols.

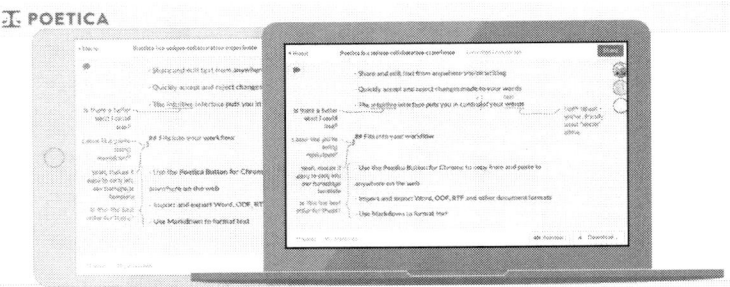

Poetica's cloud-based editing tool lets you use traditional copy editing marks.

I also recently discovered Grammarly, a spelling and grammar checker plus plagiarism tool that automatically checks for errors as you write in Microsoft Word (Windows only for now) and online in WordPress, PressBooks, Facebook, and other social media sites.

Google Drive, an office suite in the cloud, offers Google docs, spreadsheets, and other tools that work much like those in the Microsoft Word suite. Google Drive gives you 15MG of storage free, but for an additional $5 a month you get 100GB more to store, sync, and share documents, images, videos, and other data, accessing it from any of your devices. This is a really good deal and it's great for backups and for sharing your work. You can download your doc from Google Drive to Word and use a template to create your ebooks and PDF for print.

You can also create an ebook in EPUB directly from Google Drive (or Dropbox, OneDrive, or Github), using a simple but innovative cloud-based program called Liberio. This is a very quick, simple way to create ebooks. It's not perfect, but it's a great solution for drafts and beta readers.

I wasn't going to mention Calibre and Sigil because they're a little geeky for the average self-publishing author, but they appear in search engines so often when authors are looking for formatting and conversion, I thought you should know about them. Calibre is an open source ebook creation tool that exports your book to all the ebook formats. Sigil simply creates EPUBs. They're both rather complicated, but many authors like them. I don't know why since there are so many other simpler solutions. If you like these tools, perhaps you can tell me what situation you use them in, or what they do that PressBooks, Joel's templates, and Scrivener don't do. Please contact me.

Your favorites?

So these are my favorite tools and the ones I use most often during the book creation and formatting process. I hope you'll want to add a few of these tools to your writing and publishing toolkit. Which ones will you explore? What have I missed, what are your favorites, and how do you use them? I'd love to hear from you! ♥

Find a complete list of resources and information on virtual Self-Pub Boot Camp workshops at
www.SelfPubBootCamp.com/resources.

CHAPTER TWO

YOUR PUBLISHING PATH

In this chapter, I've tried to identify your best publishing choices. I know you'll be able to apply one or a combination of techniques to your particular scenario. There are so many ways to publish, and I know it can be overwhelming. But it pays to take your time during this first step, carefully researching the capabilities of the vendors you are considering. I know many authors who have hurried through this process and are sorry later.

There is no one-size fits all solution. Many overlap and the price structures, though fair, can be complex. Some services are free, others charge fees. For those that charge for their services, some require a setup fee and others take a percentage of your book sales. Some refund your setup fee after you order a number of books. Some services reach only one sales channel; others reach many. Some provide digital distribution only, others print only, and some offer both digital and print formatting plus wide distribution.

There are all kinds of pros and cons to using a combination of services and other arguments for using a full-service vendor. If you're on a very tight budget, you'll be attracted to the free services. If you have money, you can hire a publishing pro to handle all this for you. Even so, it pays to be aware of the publishing landscape so you can work intelligently with your consultants.

You really can't go wrong if you stick to my list of trusted vendors. I update this list constantly for my email newsletter subscribers as vendors change their services and business models, and as I become aware of and test, new tools and services. I rely on you, the author, for recommendations, too, so I'd love your input on any of these paths, products, and services.

- Retailer-specific tools
- Creating your ebook
- Distributing your ebook
- Creating your print book
- Distributing your print book
- Services that distribute both ebooks and print
- Reader subscription programs
- Independent book formatting services

- Hybrid publishing
- Traditional distribution
- Book packagers
- Book producers
- Printing companies
- Literary agents
- Vanity and subsidy presses

Retailer-specific tools

You may want to test the waters for your ebook by uploading it to a single vendor first. These online retailers want your business and have created tools that make it easy to reach their stores. The two I recommend the most for testing books is Amazon CreateSpace for experimenting with your print book and Smashwords (standard catalog) for testing out your ebook. But I wanted you to know about the others, too.

- Amazon CreateSpace
- Amazon Kindle Direct Publishing (KDP)
- Amazon Kindle Kids' Book Creator
- Apple iBooks Author
- B&N Nook Press
- Kobo Writing Life
- Smashwords

You can reach all of these stores and more with "big" distribution through Smashwords, IngramSpark, BookBaby, Blurb, Bowker, and others.

Creating your ebook

There are lots of ways to create an ebook in EPUB, Kindle, and fixed-layout formats. Some vendors offer do-it-yourself tools and some do-it-for-you, others offer both options. Some are simple to use and create only simple books, and others offer complex and flexible applications to use to create astoundingly complex books verging on games. Here are the ebook creation tools and services I recommend most often.

- Aerbook
- BookBaby
- Bowker
- IngramSpark
- Joel Friedlander's book design templates
- PressBooks
- Scrivener

Distributing your ebook

Once you create your ebook, you can distribute it using these vendors. Most offer ebook formatting and conversion services or, in the case of Smashwords and Blurb, a list of professionals who can help you.

- Aerbook
- Blurb
- BookBaby
- Bowker

- IngramSpark
- Smashwords

Creating your print book

Creating a print book requires that you format it to standard print book sizes and provide a PDF file to the printer. It's easy to create a PDF, but it's not so easy to create a beautiful book. Here are the tools and services that will help you. Some are do-it-yourself, and some services do it for you.

- Aerbook
- Blurb
- BookBaby
- CreateSpace
- IngramSpark
- Joel Friedlander's book design templates
- PressBooks
- Scrivener

By the way, it doesn't matter how you print—POD, offset or short run—you always need a PDF. The spine width may slightly differ with each printer as their paper weights and bulk differ, so you may need to make adjustments to the cover art.

Distributing your print book

Once you create your PDF for print, you can upload your book for sale on the online retailers websites. Here are services that distribute your book to large and small online retailers, and a couple of them can give you access to brick-and-mortar bookstores. Some of them also offer print book creation services.

- Blurb
- BookBaby
- CreateSpace
- IngramSpark

Services that distribute both print and ebooks

These are the services I like that distribute both your ebook and your print book to the online retailers and brick-and-mortar bookstores. Each offers a unique set of do-it-yourself or do-it-for-you services to help you create your book, or you can supply them with pre-formatted book files.

- Blurb
- BookBaby
- IngramSpark

Reader subscription programs

I mention subscription programs separately to help you determine which ebook distribution service you might want to use to reach them. You'll read more about each of these in the next chapter.

- Kindle Unlimited via Amazon KDP Select
- Oyster via Smashwords or BookBaby
- Scribd via Smashwords or BookBaby

Independent book formatting services

Hire an ebook conversion professional or service to ensure a perfectly formatted version of your book in all the different formats, guaranteed. The cost for a book containing mostly text ranges from about $100 to $350. The more complex your book is, the higher the cost. If the person or company your hire manages the files with the online retailers, that also costs something, but you may find the convenience worth the price. Find updated recommendations for conversion services in my writing and publishing email newsletter.

Heavily formatted books need a personal touch to look perfect in each ebook format. Ebook formatting companies quickly learn how to format for new hardware and your book can be offered early in the market on those devices.

Once you receive your formatted ebook files, you can manage your relationships with each ebook retailer individually, uploading to each store, agreeing to terms, and entering metadata, banking information, and other data. Or send your files to a distributor to centralize this task.

You may not need to hire an independent formatting service if you like the packages that companies like BookBaby and Bowker offer. They do a great job of formatting at a great price and they also distribute your book. Very complex books will cost more, either way, and you may enjoy the one-on-one relationship with a formatter you hire. If you want to try to create a complex book yourself, I recommend Blurb's BookWright tool.

There are so many independent book formatting services companies out there today that I can't even begin to list them here. (I do keep a running list for my email newsletter subscribers.) Good ones will do a meticulous job of making sure that your book looks absolutely perfect on all devices. Some churn out standard EPUB and MOBI ebooks and others specialize in highly formatted books with tables, mathematical formulas, images, and complex page layouts for viewing on the tablet computers. Get a recommendation from another author or find a list in my friend Joel Friedlander's Self-Publisher's Ultimate Resource Guide. (See the back of this book for more recommended books and sites.)

Hybrid publishing

The term "hybrid," above any other, typifies the last two years of publishing. As traditional publishing declined, the tools and services for authors became so plentiful, so simple and so affordable that frustrated authors flocked to self-publishing. Finally, traditional publishers stopped turning up their noses at self-published titles and started making offers on the bestsellers. Sometimes indie authors accepted, but more and more often they said, "Why would I?"

The fall of the traditional publishing empire left a lot of people out of work who are now freelancing. Book distributors, printing companies, small presses, packagers, and even literary agents have morphed their services to serve indie authors in order to sustain their businesses.

These kinds of businesses are much more agile than the Big 5 publishing companies. They're creative in their dealings with authors, offering a range of services. Some will happily take your money to produce (edit, design, format) and distribute your book, but others will look for a long term investment in you as an author. You'll need to woo this type of partner with a book proposal and business plan. It will help you clarify your own goals for your book, as outlined in my chapter on doing business as an author. (You may also benefit from my colleague Nina Amir's course on How to Craft a Proposal for a Book that Sells.)

There is no one typical hybrid publishing model. Below I've provided a list of a few businesses to give you an idea of the variety and scope of services and partnerships available. It's worth noting that all of these businesses are located in the San Francisco Bay Area, which is a hotbed of publishing innovation and technology. My reportage may be skewed because my experience is in the Bay Area, too. Please let me know if you know of other great models for indie publishers. Here are the examples I promised:

Fuse Literary is a full-service, hybrid literary agency led by Laurie McLean, a former Silicon Valley PR professional turned literary agent. Fuse offers a blend of traditional publishing for authors of fiction and nonfiction for children and adults. They manage a wide variety of clients and offer "technical efficiency with outside-the-covers creative thinking so that each individual client's career is specifically fine-tuned for them."

She Writes Press is a hybrid publisher focusing on writing by women, founded to serve as a platform for authors who don't have one so that they can legitimately compete with their traditional counterparts. They are a small press with a curated list, but they also offer editing and coaching services to authors they don't publish.

Hyperink is an ebook-only publisher who seeks experts, especially bloggers, to create books from their existing materials for a 50/50 revenue split.

InkShares is a publisher crowdfunding platform that helps authors raise money for their books and publishes them under fairly traditional terms though with more generous revenue sharing (50%-70% royalty).

As I said, these are just a few of the models under the wide category of hybrid publishing: small presses, crowd-funding platforms, literary agents, and blog-to-book publishers. All very creative. Got more examples? I'd love to hear about them!

Traditional distribution

"How do I get traditional distribution?" is a common question of many indie authors. But I often answer, "Do you really want it?" Distributors will probably take 65% or more of your book's profits and insist on exclusivity, which may mean that you can't sell your own book. Not online, not even from your own website. If you have a speaking engagement you can purchase books from your distributor at half price. This is not unfair as they put a lot of labor into selling your book.

That said, I know lots of authors who print books in quantity with an offset print vendor and use a distributor to sell them. These authors have written books specifically to boost their business or enhance their careers. In other words, they don't expect to make money from the book but they expect the book to make money for their business. They look at the book as an investment.

For example, my friend Allan Karl, a successful business owner in San Diego, was burnt out, newly divorced and needed a break. So he sold everything and set off on a life-changing round-the-world solo motorcycle journey. During the years-long trip, he connected with lots of people, mostly over food. Allan is a great photographer and graphic artist and his book, *FORKS: A Quest for Culture, Cuisine, and Connection*, is a luscious full-color hardback travelogue and cookbook that took much more time and money to produce than he ever hoped to make back in book sales. But he's a great marketer and the extremely high quality of *FORKS*, paired with his natural enthusiasm, landed him on television around the USA, including on big shows like Good Morning America. Consequently, his keynote speaking career has soared.

Allan chose Small Press United (SPU) to distribute his book. SPU is a division of Independent Publishers Group created specifically to serve serious indie authors and start-up small presses. If you're one of the fewer than

20% of authors accepted into their program they will present your book to resellers right next to offerings from the mainstream press. They can also print your book on-demand and format your ebook.

But don't overlook the smaller distribution companies, some of whom may have very narrow specialties—for example, a company that specializes in spiritual titles or romance or regional books. These niche distributors and hybrid presses are easier to find if you're a member of an organization like the Independent Book Publishers Association (IBPA)—the largest not-for-profit trade association in the book publishing industry—which not only lists author services and distributors, but have author members who can recommend them (or not).

Book packagers

Larry Jacobson, another traveler friend, chose to outsource the production and distribution of his book to a packager. *The Boy Behind the Gate* is about Larry's escape from the rat-race by buying a sailboat and traveling the world. Like Allan, Larry makes a living today as an inspirational speaker and business coach.

Book packagers do everything except marketing and promotion. They print, format your ebook, fulfill and distribute. This is expensive and the fees can really pile up, but again, if you're using a book to enhance your speaking career, business or promote professional services, it can be worth the investment to free yourself to concentrate on your revenue-generating business.

As with a distributor, your deal with a book packager may be exclusive and you must buy your books from them (at a discount) if you want to sell on your own website or at an event.

Book producers

A book producer can manage your entire publishing project from beginning to end. They know how to do things like buy ISBNs, format books, manage metadata, and create Amazon author pages. They'll have access to a stable of editors and designers, web developers, and other pros, and can teach you how to use social media. They can help you with or completely take over all the production functions that a literary agent or publishing house might traditionally do for you. In fact, there are lots of book production pros who used to work at traditional publishing houses. You can find them in all price ranges. Make sure to get recommendations and samples of their work, and also make sure you like each other. You'll work very closely together.

Printing companies

In the past few years, I've seen more and more printing companies offer publishing services, including editing and design, ebook creation and distribution. Though these companies are truly experts in printing and distribution, many are large and conservative, lacking the agility of high-tech's faster adoption of tech and partnerships. I haven't yet seen any printing companies who can truly compete with the services of the hybrid publishers I know. Have you? Please let me know!

Literary agents

Many of today's literary agents offer more than agenting services. Before you sign a contract with an agent, it's important to understand the various roles they might play in helping you publish.

Agent: An agent is an individual or firm who represents your work and negotiates with publishers to obtain the best possible advance and royalty. An agent's fee is about 15% of your net profit. An agent who has sold your book might offer to help you self-publish other materials to boost sales.

Publishing Consultant: An agent or agency might act as publishing consultant, book producer, or coach, offering for-fee services to handle editing, design, formatting and other tasks. If you find it tedious to hire individuals, you might find it easier to centralize activities with one publishing pro. Agents are often well connected with a network of very good editors, designers, ebook formatters and publicity professionals. They'll also handle tasks like buying ISBNs, registering copyright and optimizing your book website.

Publisher: Many agencies have even formed their own in-house publishing companies. Earlier I mentioned Laurie McLean's agency, Fuse Literary, as an example of a hybrid publisher. Laurie helped me understand how the agent-publisher roles can conflict, and advises authors to be wary of agents who take your book on in the agent role and then offer you self-publishing services or publication for a fee, which is quite a different role. So before employing an agency be clear on the role and relationship between you and the company.

Vanity presses

I present the topic of vanity presses as a warning, not a recommendation so that you can recognize them.

In general, vanity presses make money from selling services to you, and not from selling your books. They charge lots of money for services and also make a good amount of profit by charging you much more to print your book. For example, I can buy this book, the one you're reading now, in print from CreateSpace at about $3 a copy, plus postage. With a vanity (or subsidy) press, my cost per book will be over $6. Plus they would charge me hundreds, if not thousands, for a publishing package.

These companies make a lot of promises, offering basic to deluxe packages, with some of them are priced into the five-figures. They say they'll help you with all aspects of book development—editing, design, marketing, ebook conversion, copyright, returns programs, and distribution, and they will, maybe even competently, but for a much higher price that you need to pay.

These companies make money in two ways, by selling you expensive services and by selling your own books to you at inflated print costs. You have probably already heard that the great majority of authors sell fewer than 200 books, and most of those are to friends and family. The fact that these companies make a profit (Author Solutions, Inc. to the tune of about $100 million a year) speaks to the number of authors they attract and the amount of money they charge for their services.

Here's how to identify vanity presses: They sell high-priced "packages." They do not allow you to assign your own ISBN. They have a large enough marketing budget that their name pops up again and again and again in ads and search engines. They use language like "your book deserves to be published," "tell the story that needs to be told," and "imagine your book on the shelf at your local bookstore." They offer add-ons that claim to get your book in front of literary agents and movie producers. This might be true, but I don't know who these agents and producers are or what they've produced.

When a company, and not you, owns the ISBN for your book, your book is effectively trapped with that company. This is okay if you have a partner publisher who is truly invested in your book's success. But again, a vanity press concentrates on selling you the highest-priced package they can, and they'll keep selling to you as long as they can.

Authors who do their due diligence almost always identify these companies and avoid them. But many authors are so anxious to publish that they buy the sales pitch—hook, line, and sinker. All the companies owned by Author Solutions, Inc., fall into this category (iUniverse, Author House, Trafford, Xlibris, Balboa, Archway, Westbow, and more), but there are many others. Do your research. ♥

My audio-video presentations for Self-Pub Boot Camp focus on the publishing path. For more on the virtual workshops and a complete list of resources, please visit www.SelfPubBootCamp.com/resources.

CHAPTER THREE

TRUSTED VENDORS

In the first two chapters of this book, I describe the author's toolset and possible publishing paths available to you through the entire lifecycle of your book. As you've seen, you can do everything yourself, essentially for free—if you don't count your labor costs—or you can hire out services for a few hundred to a few thousand dollars.

Today, in 2015, my list of trusted vendors is fairly stable, but new ones are always popping up, and the old favorites continually improve their services with new features and sales channels. (Though, in one case a service removed features to concentrate on doing just one thing better.) Please join my email newsletter to stay up to date with what's going on.

Please note that I am an affiliate of a few of these products or programs, which means I earn a small percentage of sales if you visit and buy using my link. I only seek out connections with people, products, and companies I have used, love and recommend. (Don't know what an affiliate is? Check out Wikipedia's page on affiliate marketing.) Thanks for clicking!

- Aerbook and Aer.io
- Amazon CreateSpace
- Amazon Kindle Direct Publishing (KDP)
- Amazon Kindle Kids Books Creator
- Blurb
- Book Design Templates
- BookBaby
- Bowker
- GoDaddy
- Gumroad
- IngramSpark
- Leanpub
- Lightning Source
- MailChimp
- PressBooks
- Scribd
- Scrivener
- Slicebooks
- Smashwords
- WordPress
- Your trusted tools?

Aerbook and Aer.io

Aerbook founder Ron Martinez is a digital publishing futurist who is always dreaming up cool new tools for authors. His first product was Aerbook Maker, an easy to use, full-color multimedia ebook creator in the cloud.

But Aerbook's greatest value is in marketing and selling your book. Aerbook's tiered products (Retail, Plus, and Flyer) were designed to help you share and even sell your books on the social web (Facebook, Twitter, Pinterest). Upload your book and share a preview with your friends, launching it into your social stream where your friends will, ideally, share it with their friends, and so on, in a non-salesy or spammy way.

What's truly wonderful about this is that readers can preview your book directly without leaving the social media site, and then buy via the Aerbook online sales channel or an online retailer, whichever you choose. Martinez says the idea is to reach readers where they already are, instead of making them leave their comfort zone to navigate to a URL.

Martinez's new brainstorm for 2015 is Aer.io (now in beta), a tool that gives you the ability to easily and profitably sell books, video, audio and related merchandise on any website, and directly within social streams and apps.

You can curate books as an indie publisher with an online bookstore. So, imagine that your site curates historical fiction based in 18th century France, or the Enneagram personality type indicator, or computer books related to Ruby on Rails. These are incredibly niche topics but, when you curate as well as sell your own—well, I think it's a great marketing strategy, not to mention the benefits of an additional income stream. It also might inspire you to gather a group of authors together to create a shared online retail space. I can dream up profitable uses for both fiction and nonfiction authors with Aer.io.

Amazon CreateSpace

Use Amazon CreateSpace to create, proof, and distribute your book directly to the Amazon.com bookstore. Even if you're not going to use CreateSpace for distribution, it's a great tool for simply proofreading and testing out various book designs. They offer quick turnaround, great customer service by real people in the USA that you can reach by phone, the lowest-cost POD service I've found, and there's no setup fee.

CreateSpace offers book design templates, but I don't recommend them as Joel Friedlander's book design templates and PressBooks themes are so much more beautiful and professional looking.

To print proofs, or advance reader copies (ARCs)—more on ARCs in the chapter on marketing and promotion—create and upload PDFs of your book interior and cover according to their instructions. Keep the book private, and order copies sent to you. If you don't like it, experiment! Edit the cover, change the fonts, make revisions and corrections. Upload the book again, order another copy, and proof it once more. This is the magic of POD. You can repeat this process as many times as you like until you are happy with your book.

Your book sells in the CreateSpace store for 80% royalty, but it won't get lots of visibility there, so make sure to sell it in the Amazon store where the book buyers shop.

If you have not already created your Kindle version, you can pay Amazon about $70 to create a KDP-formatted ebook file for sale in the Kindle store.

Amazon Kindle Direct Publishing (KDP)

Like CreateSpace, Amazon Kindle Direct Publishing (KDP's) sole purpose is to distribute your ebook to a single channel: Amazon. You'll need a KDP account and a specially-formatted MS Word doc file, which is almost identical to the Smashwords format. So if you already have a Smashwords edition, just make a copy, give it a new ISBN, and make adjustments as spelled out in the

KDP formatting guidelines. (Or vice-versa, you can copy your KDP file and modify it for Smashwords. But be sure to check instructions in the free Smashwords Style Guide or hire someone from Mark's List, see below.)

If you're starting from scratch, the KDP book formatting guidelines are fairly easy to follow. If your book is already for sale in the Amazon CreateSpace store, the Amazon Kindle Conversion Service team will create your file for $79. Of course, if you use a template or service to create your files, you won't have to worry about this step.

If you're a publishing geek, you probably already know that in 2014 Amazon started to replace MOBI with Kindle Format 8 (KF8). If you use KindleGen or the Kindle Previewer program to create your Kindle ebook, it will now create a KF8 book. KF8 was developed for the new Kindle Fire tablets, and it also works with 4th-generation devices by Kindle for PC and Kindle Reader for the Mac.

You might have heard of KDP Select, Amazon's exclusive program that many authors use to give their book a boost during launch, hoping for bestseller status in a particular category. In exchange for exclusivity Amazon will give you marketing perks. Some people love this program, others believe that any exclusivity is detrimental to book sales. I'm in the latter camp. But, as always, it's up to you to develop your marketing strategy.

Amazon Kindle Kids' Book Creator

Amazon Kindle Kids' Book Creator launched in 2014 as a tool for indie authors to easily create and sell children's books to owners of Kindle Fire tablets. The authors I know who have used it say that it's still pretty basic, but I expect improvements and enhancements through 2015. This is the only way to create a children's book for the Kindle Fire, other than doing it yourself or hiring a professional KF8 designer.

Blurb

Blurb is a full color book print and ebook creation service that will print your POD or offset print book to sell in their store and to distribute when you're ready. Their BookWright tool creates fixed-layout EPUB files at the same time you're building your print book, which is pretty awesome. In exchange for using these awesome tools they do lock you into their distribution service which is a fair price in my opinion for making it really simple for you. A getaround is buying your own PDF and EPUB files for a reasonable price, if you want to print and distribute elsewhere, but you may not want to.

I've often recommended that authors with complex, full-color books create books with Blurb as a test run for designers, advance review copies, or for sale to a niche audience. (Weddings! Family reunions! Puppies!) As with CreateSpace, you can order one copy at a time until you're happy with it. Then decide if you want Blurb to handle fulfillment and distribution to Amazon and the Ingram distribution network. Many do. *{I am a Blurb affiliate.}*

Book Design Templates

As you may have already noticed, I can't say enough good things about Joel Friedlander's book design templates for book creation in Word and InDesign, not to mention his media kit for your website, press release template, book proposal template, and other products. These tools offload a lot of the hard work of design and rote work by providing do-it-for-you products and services for very reasonable prices.

All the major book distribution companies accept these templates, including CreateSpace, IngramSpark, BookBaby and Smashwords.

I wrote more about the templates in the previous chapter on essential tools for indie authors. Find out more and buy the templates by visiting the SelfPubBootCamp.com

Resources page. *{I am an affiliate of Joel Friedlander's book design templates and other products.}*

BookBaby

BookBaby can format and distribute just about any kind of book you want to throw at them in both ebook and print formats. They recently unveiled their own print-on-demand (POD) program for self published authors. Unlike most distribution services, they don't just contract distribution out to Ingram but have organized their own deals to supplement Ingram distribution. For example, somehow, amazingly, they have figured out how to reach bricks and-mortar bookstores without that awful returns program we've all suffered with these long years.

In all, BookBaby distributes ebooks and printed books to well over 100 bookstores, wholesale book catalogs and sales networks. They distribute to all the major online retailers like Amazon, Barnes & Noble, Powell's, the Ingram catalog (38,000 retailers and libraries), the full Baker & Taylor catalog, and dozens of niche and international book distributors and retail outlets. Don't worry, there's no conflict or cross-channel selling here, they've worked it out for you.

As for their pricing structure, instead of taking a percentage of sales they charge authors a flat fee ($299 for ebooks only, add $199 for POD) to convert and distribute your book. Then you keep 100% of net sales (after the sales channels have taken their percentage).

Their main package provides conversion and distribution, 25 printed books and POD distribution for around $579. They also offer cover design for $149 (basic) or $279 (deluxe).

BookBaby will happily accept your pre-formatted files or you can send them your existing EPUB file, an MS Word doc file, or if you only have a PDF, InDesign, or Quark file, they will convert it from those formats, too. As a multimedia company, they can help create enhanced ebooks, too, and produce a handful of specialty projects each month that include audio, video, mastering and authoring.

I've watched BookBaby grow over the years and have admired their dedication to service indie authors. Disc Makers, the company that owns BookBaby, also serves indie musicians and filmmakers with CDBaby. Their HostBaby website builder is an easy-to-use content management system.

If you're an author without a website (yet, and I hope you're planning one), BookBaby provides a free e-commerce page through their BookShop service. As with the CreateSpace and Blurb stores, you earn more royalty by selling direct than via distribution, though of course your book will not be nearly as visible to customers as generally that's not where they shop. *{I am a BookBaby affiliate.}*

Bowker

Bowker is the official U.S. ISBN agency and you should buy your own set of 10 or more here. (Other countries have similar agencies.) They also offer self-publishing solutions for digital book creation and distribution. Navigate to their My Identifiers service to explore the options.

Ebook conversion (from Word doc to EPUB and MOBI) starts at a very reasonable $139 for simple books. (They outsource conversion to Data Conversion Laboratory, Inc., a company that formats books for big publishing, that self-publishers cannot reach except via Bowker.) They also provide creation and distribution services along with 10 ISBNs for under $500 with their Self-Publisher Prime program. It's a good deal.

I'm not convinced that the QR codes and "look inside" widgets they offer are worth the money, but they're high-quality options to freebies that you get elsewhere. I discuss Bowker and ISBNs in more detail in the chapters on your publishing business and metadata and discovery.

GoDaddy

I've used GoDaddy to buy domain names for years and also to host my websites with their Managed WordPress Hosting, and as my email provider. The advantages of Managed WordPress hosting over plain, self-hosted WordPress is described in more detail in my chapter on websites and blogs.

GoDaddy has always had great customer service, great pricing on domain names, hosting and email. Coincidentally, my brother Jeff took a position running the web hosting division a while back, and I think he's doing a great job. But my satisfaction in working with the company predates his employment there.

Gumroad

Gumroad offers a vibrant online store and provides widgets to embed in your site. You can even allow fans to pre-order your product. As with crowdfunding platforms, buyer's cards are charged on the release date and ebooks are digitally downloaded automatically. For existing products, simply upload and sell your digital files—up to 4 GB—or create an order form for selling physical objects. Integrated Facebook and Twitter buttons encourage sharing with customer networks. You get customer data and 95% royalty minus a 25¢ transaction fee.

I like Gumroad for its ability to provide both digital downloads and order forms for physical products, as an easy shopping cart system for your site and features that help authors drum up excitement during the book launch.

IngramSpark

Ingram is the giant in the traditional book distribution world and the independent publishing world as well. Generally, if you want your book sold by your local bookseller or to libraries, they need to be able to order it from Ingram. In total, Ingram boasts 38,000 retail and library partners and has long served as the center hub in book publishing and distribution for every company involved in the process.

IngramSpark is Ingram's simplified tool for self-publishers and small press, and a great alternative to Lightning Source (LSI), which is the engine that runs IngramSpark. So if you don't already work with LSI, use IngramSpark instead.

IngramSpark lets you set the higher discounts and returns programs that brick-and-mortar bookstores require. So if you're sure that you have a market in these stores, and you're willing to do the promotion work to reach them, IngramSpark (or LSI) can be a great choice. You can set discounts on print titles from 30% and 55%

to attract brick-and-mortar bookstores *and* sell to markets that allow you to take more of the profit.

An advantage of IngramSpark to authors who travel and sell books in other parts of the world is their ability to print your books on-demand to those locations and have them sent to your destination using local postage rates.

When you print with IngramSpark your $49 print (POD) setup fee is deducted and refunded after you order 50 books. This is a reasonable number of books to order for gifts and publicity. So essentially, if you buy 50 books (and I think you will), you can compare this vendor to the many free services out there.

It's also important to understand that IngramSpark pays 40% of *list price* (rather than *sales price*). Sales price is calculated on the price that the retailer sells your book for on their site, so the profit you make will depend on the discounted price on any given day. When you're paid based on the list price you consistently get the same profit on each sale.

If your self-published author business grows into a small press, IngramSpark can move you into Ingram Publisher Services (IPS), which provides full distribution services including warehousing and sales into major and independent booksellers.

By now you are probably wondering how to choose a book creation and distribution service and we're not even halfway through the list! Well, Ingram has a huge distribution network but BookBaby has managed to create their own effective distribution network that reaches brick-and-mortar stores, too. IngramSpark lets you opt out of the Amazon Kindle and Apple iBooks stores, and BookBaby allows you to pick and choose from all their retailers and territories. They both provide print and ebook distribution and centralized metadata and sales information. The biggest difference is in their book creation services. BookBaby can do all the design and formatting for you, and IngramSpark provides (later in 2015) a cloud-based tool so you can do this yourself. Blurb, another competitor, also provides DIY book creation services with an outstanding product called BookWright that helps you build complex, fixed-layout ebooks and print books, and also uses Ingram's distribution network.

No matter what tool you use, you'll probably end up paying about the same amount of money. So decide if you prefer a full-service option or you want more control by doing it yourself using book design templates and hiring out cover design. I hope all this information and distinctions make it easier for you to choose between more control and hands-on involvement or hiring more of the process out to a single vendor.

Leanpub

With Leanpub, you can quickly publish beta books, books in progress, serials, and subscriptions, updating your readers automatically when the book is updated. You can also pay a co-author automatically and set up a donation to a cause.

Create your book using simple Markdown language (an easy, plain-text format), then upload it to a connected Dropbox folder along with images and other assets. (This may sound a little complicated but they do much of it for you automatically, and provide easy instructions.)

As with PressBooks, your book lives in the cloud, so you can make it available to trusted editors, collaborators, and assistants who can edit and replace files. A publisher page holds common assets like a verso page, copyright message, company logo and other elements that can be applied to more than one book. Take advantage of pay-what-you-want pricing by setting a minimum and suggested price, such as $4.99–$10.99, or even higher. Leverage your *1000 True Fans* by asking for donations up to $500.

I think Leanpub is a very overlooked and underused tool in the general indie publishing marketplace. Especially as you can make money with your writing before your book is done, plus leverage your readers to beta test your book and give you feedback of all sorts, from developmental editing to detailed proofreading to instructional corrections or just encouragement.

Lightning Source

See IngramSpark.

MailChimp

MailChimp is an email marketing service provider that helps you collect email addresses from interested website visitors, and is possibly your most important marketing tool. Other vendors that do the same thing include Constant Contact, Vertical Response and AWeber. You can use MailChimp for free if your list is under 2000 email addresses. They make it easy to place a signup form on your website and blog. *{I am a MailChimp affiliate.}*

PressBooks

PressBooks is an online publishing tool that produces beautifully-designed PDFs that you can distribute in print and ebook formats using vendors like BookBaby, CreateSpace, and IngramSpark, or any of the digital-only services.

PressBooks is built on the open source WordPress blogging platform so, if you're blogging on WordPress, you already know how to use it. In fact, PressBooks is a great blog-to-book tool. I wrote a detailed, step-by-step tutorial for my friend Nina Amir, who is the blog-to-book queen and author of a very inspiring and useful book titled *How to Blog a Book*. Blogging a book is a very public effort and it is a great way to hold yourself accountable. A new expanded edition of Nina's book is due mid-2015 and available for pre-order.)

I've created several books and booklets with PressBooks, including this one. I think you should consider it an essential part of your author toolset. It's also wonderful for creating short books to give away on your website as an enticement to sign up for your email newsletter. For example, my MotoSFO Guide to Northern California Wine Country was a giveaway for one of my (now defunct) motorcycle travel websites.

PressBooks sends their customers to BookBaby for print and ebook distribution. You could just as well use CreateSpace and IngramSpark plus Smashwords and KDP, too. They're all great and so you'll need to determine which vendors are best matched to your skillset and the work you want to do yourself, the amount of control you want to keep and the various pricing and distribution models.

Scribd

I've long used Scribd to share stories and beta-launch books. Basically it's a document sharing site that lets you sell or give away your stories, excerpts and ebooks in PDF and document formats. There's lots of platform-building potential here as commenting, social media and sharing widgets are everywhere. It's free to join and their take is 20% of sales plus a 25¢ transaction fee.

The company differentiated itself early on from other document sharing sites by specifically serving the author community and developing the sales, distribution and publishing side of their business. Today Scribd is focused on their very successful reader subscription program that competes with Kindle Unlimited and Oyster. I wrote more about subscription programs in a post for PBS MediaShift.

Though the social publishing features are not as prominent as they once were, I still describe Scribd is as kind of a Wattpad for grownups, with the bonus of being able to sell your work and distribute private beta docs.

Scrivener

Scrivener is one of my favorite tools and you can find more information about it in the previous chapter about essential tools. It's a desktop writing and organization app with an amazing feature set that can help you develop stories and books. Last year I started using it to organize and write my blog posts, articles, and books and I don't know how I lived without it all this time. There's a 30 day free trial, and you can buy Scrivener for Windows or Mac. *{I am a Scrivener affiliate.}*

Slicebooks

Upload your books into Slicebooks to slice and dice them into chapters and sections. Remix your catalog into completely new titles with new covers and sell them in an iTunes style retail platform. You can also offer the slices for sale separately.

Consumers can mix and match slices with any other slice sold in the Slicebooks store. Embed your own store to offer your content sliced and remixable. You're paid by the slice, too. Travel books? Anthologies? Cookbooks? Imagine the possibilities.

Slice your books to create new ones or offer customers slices of your book to mix and match with other publisher's slices.

Smashwords

If you've written a simple, text-heavy ebook, the fastest and cheapest way to get it distributed quickly is to pair Smashwords with Amazon Kindle Direct Publishing

(KDP). This do-it-yourself option requires some Microsoft Word formatting skill or a Word template like one offered by Joel Friedlander. Upload your book to both services (use a different ISBN for each), and you've got quick and complete ebook distribution as Smashwords distributes everywhere but to the Amazon Kindle store.

Smashwords makes your book readable on any e-reading device, including the Amazon Kindle, the Apple iPhone/iPod Touch/iPad, the Sony Reader, the Barnes & Noble Nook, personal computers, and mobile devices.

You receive 85% of the net sales proceeds from your titles (about 70% for affiliate sales), and 60% of the list price for all sales through major retailers. Though Smashwords makes your book available in the Kindle format, it does not distribute to the Kindle store.

I want to include some verbiage from the Smashwords Distribution page to give you an idea of the kind of distribution they offer, partly through Ingram but with additional reach such as to the app stores.

> *Once your book is accepted into the Premium Catalog, we automatically distribute it to major online retailers such as Apple (distribution to iBooks stores in 51 countries), Barnes & Noble (US and UK), Scribd, Oyster, Kobo, OverDrive (world's largest library ebook platform serving 20,000+ libraries), Flipkart (New September 29, 2013: India's largest online bookseller), Baker & Taylor (Blio and the Axis360 library service), Page Foundry (operates retail sites*

> *Inktera.com and Versent.com; and operates Android ebook store apps for Cricket Wireless and Asus), and other distribution outlets coming soon. Additionally, Kobo powers the ebook stores of multiple ebook retailers around the world. Simply by distributing to Kobo via Smashwords, your books will also reach WH Smith in the UK, FNAC in France and Portugul, Livraria Cultura in Brazil, Angus & Robertson in Australia, Bookworld in Australia, Indigo in Canada, Collins in Australia, Feltrinelli in Italy, Libris in the Netherlands, Paper Plus in New Zealand, Play in Great Britain, Rakuten in Japan, Buy.com (now Rakuten) in the US, Whitcoulls in New Zealand, and more on the way.*

Start by formatting your MS Word doc file in compliance with founder Mark Coker's free Smashwords Style Guide. You can figure this out yourself or make it easy and use one of Joel Friedlander's book design templates, or hire someone to do it for you. Mark keeps a list of formatters and designers.

Assign a unique ISBN to the Smashwords version of your ebook and upload it to the Smashwords Premium Catalog for wide distribution. When you submit the document, the Smashwords "meatgrinder" will generate versions of your book in all the important formats to be aggregated in most of the major online retailers.

Once your book is successfully converted, Smashwords offers it for sale immediately on their site, and then sends it to the major ebook sellers—except the Amazon Kindle store. You'll need to upload a separate file (with a differ-

TRUSTED VENDORS

ent ISBN) to the Kindle store via Amazon's Kindle Direct Publishing. (Find out more on ISBNs in the chapters on your publishing business and metadata and discovery.)

Royalties from Smashwords are defined as follows. (Again, from the Smashwords Distribution page.)

> ...publishers earn 85% or more of the net proceeds from the sale of their works. Net proceeds to author = (sales price minus PayPal payment processing fees)*.85 for sales at Smashwords.com, our retail operation. Authors receive 70.5% for affiliate sales. Smashwords distributes books to most of the major retailers, including Apple iBooks, Barnes & Noble, Sony, Kobo and the Diesel eBook Store. Sales originated by retailers earn authors/publishers 60% of the list price. To put these high royalty rates in perspective, it means if an author has a book they might otherwise publish via a traditional commercial publisher as a $8.00 mass market paperback, which would earn a 40 cent royalty, they could publish the same book at Smashwords as an ebook and earn up to $6.45, or 16 times more. Or, they could price their ebook on Smashwords for $3.99 and make nearly 8 times the per unit amount compared to selling a traditionally published print book.

Smashwords founder Mark Coker provides lots of informational and how-to videos on their Smashwords YouTube channel.

WordPress

WordPress is web software used to create beautiful websites and blogs. It's free and open source and very popular due to its enthusiastic community of volunteers and its versatility, with thousands of plugins and themes. You really can't go wrong with a WordPress site and blog because it's easy to use and if you get stuck there are many consultants available to help at all levels and reasonable prices. PressBooks, the product I used to produce this book, is based on WordPress. My WordPress blog and website is hosted with GoDaddy, where I also buy my domain names.

Your trusted tools and services?

So these are the tools I use and trust. This list does change so to keep up to date please sign up to receive my writing and publishing news. How about you? Got suggestions and recommendations for tools and services you trust? Please let me know! ♥

TRUSTED VENDORS

My audio-video presentations for Self-Pub Boot Camp highlight trusted vendors. Many of my trusted vendors participate in the seminars, including Smashwords, BookBaby, IngramSpark, Gumroad, Blurb, Author Marketing Experts, Aerbook, Sellbox, and Wordpress Total Training. Find details on the Self-Pub Boot Camp virtual workshops and a complete list of resources at www.www.SelfPubBootCamp.com/resources.

CHAPTER FOUR

YOUR PUBLISHING BUSINESS

Self-publishers wear many hats, including that of a small business owner. This role is rewarding for many authors once they realize how much more control they have over their book than if they had sold it to a publishing company. Here are the essentials of a publishing small business to launch your first self-published book.

- Publisher name
- Fictitious business name
- Other legal and financial concerns
- Your budget
- The real cost to publish your book
- Developing a business plan
- Your mission and goals

- Raising funds
- Your sales strategy
- The Bowker record and ISBNs
- Registering your copyright
- Getting into libraries

Publisher name

Choose a name for your publishing house. This name will be displayed on your title page and the spine of your book. It may also serve as the name of your website, instead of your author name if you so choose. Think ahead and choose a name suitable for future books, products, and services. Your publisher name shouldn't scream "self-published!" but it doesn't need to sound stodgy or corporate, either. Solicit input from your friends, family, colleagues, members of your writing groups and anyone else whose opinion you value. Search the web to make sure your name isn't already taken.

Fictitious business name

If you choose a publishing house name to do business instead of your own name, you'll need a DBA (Doing Business As) in order to cash checks made out to your company name. This is also called a fictitious business name. It is a simple process, but it can take up to six weeks to complete since it requires that someone in your local government search to make sure nobody else owns the name. Then you have to advertise in a newspaper to announce your DBA.

There's no need to use expensive online services; it's a simple procedure. You can obtain DBA forms and procedures for free from your local city hall. Just fill out the forms, advertise your DBA in a local newspaper as instructed and then take your DBA paperwork to the bank to open a business account.

Other financial and legal concerns

Federal Tax ID (EIN): To separate your personal and business finances for the IRS it may be smart to obtain a Federal Employer ID (EIN) to use instead of your social security number. Get it for free from the IRS website.

Resellers Permit: If you're going to sell physical books at an event, like a conference or book show, you'll need a seller's permit or resale certificate. Sometimes event organizers will give you a temporary sellers permit. Mostly though, I've been left to my own devices, sometimes (oops!) completely forgetting about it until my tax accountant asks, and then she helps me deal with it. So make sure you figure that in and get all the paperwork you need before you sell. Just search for "sellers permit" for the state.

More legal stuff: There's lots more legal and financial stuff to know, and it can fill an entire book. Lucky for us, lawyer and self-published author Helen Sedwick has provided us with this information in her excellent Self-Publisher's Legal Handbook.

Your budget

Creating a realistic budget is important for any business. In it you'll determine what you can afford to invest in publishing your book. You'll determine your financial goals by answering the question, "Will I support the book or will the book support me?" Here's a starter list of budget items you should be aware of.

- Software and hardware
- Domain name purchases
- Web hosting services
- Mailing list management
- Blogs
- Other web-based tools
- Merchant account
- Shopping cart
- Photography
- Images and graphics
- Editing and proofreading
- DBA
- Bank fees
- POD printing

- Offset printing
- Ebook conversion
- Bowker: ISBNs, barcodes and SAN
- Book design
- Logo design
- Office supplies
- Travel expenses
- Telephone and DSL/cable expenses
- Memberships (writers and publishers organizations)
- Contest entries
- Dues and subscriptions
- Advertising
- Promotional materials
- PR services
- Review services
- Vendor fees

The real cost to publish your book

You can get ebook and print book distribution for free using a number of tools, but don't forget you need to buy your own ISBNs, which cost $295 for a set of 10. Use Mark Coker's Smashwords Style Guide to learn how to format your book for free. Better yet, ensure great formatting by using one of Joel Friedlander's book design templates, which cost roughly $50. You can also hire somebody from Mark's List for about the same amount.

Or use PressBooks to create and format your books. (Ebook $20 and ebook-plus-print for $100.) Note that IngramSpark is launching a cloud-based book-builder in Summer 2015 that will be free to use. CreateSpace has free templates in Word, but they're not nearly as good as Joel's templates or PressBooks' exports.

You can also hire book cover designers from Mark's List for $50 and up with professionals who use stock photos and basic templates and rules for each genre. But book cover design can be a very important investment in your sales so many authors will budget hundreds more. It should go without saying that you should never, ever design your own book cover. This is your biggest marketing investment.

Great do-it-for-you services include Bowker and BookBaby. The latter provides both ebook and print book creation and distribution services for $300. If you're one of those people who don't have or want to learn formatting, you'll probably take this route. For another (very reasonable) $300, BookBaby will design your book cover. So that's $600.

So at the very bare minimum I am going to bravely state that you can publish for between $300 and $1000.

However, and this is a big, "however." If you're serious about creating a quality book I think that you'll need much more help with editing, designing, marketing, and promotion, so I'm putting another zero on that number, having seen lots of authors publish beautifully for between $5,000 and $10,000.

Here's a list of some items you need to put your book respectably alongside those from traditional publishers, with minimum price tags. The lower the price, the more you have to do yourself, so bump it up if you want to be completely hands-off. Indeed, you can pay a book consultant about this much (or much more, depending on how much editing or ghostwriting and marketing is done for you).

- $1,000 Professional editing (developmental, line editing, proofreading)
- $1,000 Design (interior and cover)
- $1,000 Marketing and promotion
- $500 Advance Reading Copies (ARCs) and priority mail postage
- $500 Website design and creation (payment system, mailing list management, and related site costs)
- $500 Branding (photography, social media banners, logo, etc.)
- $300 Formatting and conversion

- $100 Membership in a professional publishers association like IBPA

But there's nothing wrong with test-driving your book using a fast, cheap, and easy method. For example, you can use Scribd or PressBooks to test drive and privately distribute your ebook. Use CreateSpace to print proofs and ARCs, ordering one at a time to evaluate the design and format, to edit and proofread—before making it available for public consumption. That's what POD is all about, after all—printing on-demand—and it can be an exciting and satisfying journey.

Developing a business plan

A business plan, even a short one, will help you with goals and expectations as it requires a look at the marketplace, competitive analysis, and financial projections.

If you are a one-book author, your business plan might consist of one simple document. If you are planning many books, or your book is tied to a product or service, it will necessarily be more complicated. There are many business plan templates on the web and in books that help.

Your mission and goals

Possibly the most valuable thing a business plan can do is to help you articulate your mission. Whenever you have to make a decision, you can return to your mission statement to help determine if the action you are about to take serves it. You may be tempted to skip this step and just blindly jump into publishing your book, but think it out, write it down and modify it as you become more aware of the challenges of becoming an author.

This step to defining your mission as an author and the goals for your book has been one of the exercises that authors have come back to me again and again to say how much it helped give them a reality check and eased their mind about writing and publishing.

For example, why are you writing this book? Is your mission to change the world, to make money, to support your business, to leave a family legacy? Your goal may be to entertain or inform a small audience—family or community—or a larger audience in a geographic area, profession, lifestyle, or interest group. Maybe you are writing to establish yourself as an expert in your field or to promote other products and services you offer. (Do you envision spinoff DVDs, workshops, a line of gourmet cookware?) Perhaps you are shooting for an international bestseller—it has been known to happen!

Perhaps you are among the many traditionally published authors disillusioned with the industry who are turning to self-publishing and creating your own small press. Or will you use your book as part of a book proposal to try to attract an agent and publisher?

Raising funds

While it may be difficult to make a living as an author, it's actually not all that hard to raise enough funds to create, produce and publish your book. You may be self-funding with your day job, or perhaps you're retired with a small income. There are other ways to raise funds, too. Pre-selling is an option and crowdfunding has enabled lots of authors to finish their books and spread their message. Preselling is rather easier than crowdfunding, which requires lots of thought, planning, and marketing.

If you have a store on your website, you can begin preselling whenever you like, and you keep the profits (minus shipping and any store merchant account fees you may incur). There are an increasing number of services that provide presales capabilities. Notable are Smashwords, Gumroad and Leanpub, all great services I recommend for other reasons besides preselling.

Smashwords and Gumroad both have pre-sales tools that let you collect credit card information from customers to be deposited on the actual date of publication.

Use Leanpub to sell your unfinished book to readers and update them when a new version is available. This is a great tool for technical and business books as well as serial books like travelogues or even fiction. This capability makes Leanpub a bit like a crowdfunding platform, as you earn money before the book is actually finished.

Author Crowdfunding

Many authors are choosing to crowdfund their work, and there are now many platforms to choose from. The most well known are Kickstarter, IndieGoGo, and Pubslush. To explore the pros and cons of each platform, I interviewed successful authors from each of them to find out why they chose it and to get tips for you from their success. Publisher-crowdfunded platforms have also cropped up and below I describe Inkshares and Unbound. The information here is adapted from my in-depth PBS MediaShift series on author crowdfunding.

Allan Karl Raised $40,994 on Kickstarter

Since Kickstarter's launch in 2009, more than 5.2 million people have pledged more than $900 million, funding nearly 53,000 creative projects like films, games, books, music, art, design and technology. Project creators set a funding goal and deadline. If people like a project, they can pledge money to make it happen. Funding on Kickstarter is all-or-nothing—projects must reach their funding goals to receive any money. To date, nearly 44% of projects have reached their funding goals. Kickstarter takes 5% of the funds raised. Funders pay via Amazon

Payments (only), which then will apply credit card processing fees (between 3% and 5%).

Kickstarter author Allan Karl took a three-year motorcycle trip around the world. Friends, family and fans followed his journey on his WorldRider blog and when he got home he wrote about it in the form of a full-color hardcover travel narrative and cookbook titled "FORKS: Three Years. Five Continents. One Motorcycle. A Quest for Culture, Cuisine, and Connection." A total of 546 backers on Kickstarter pledged $40,994—nearly double his $22,000 goal—to print and publicize the self-published book. Allan used his experience as principal of Clearcloud, a digital marketing consultancy, to create a post-journey keynote speaking career and a professional-quality coffee-table book marketed as "combining the best of Anthony Bourdain with Paul Theroux and National Geographic Adventure in a full-color, high-quality book that will bring the splendor of the world into your home and on your table."

Janna Leyde Raised $15,230 on Pubslush

Pubslush is different in that it focuses on authors. It offers flex-funding, which means you keep the money as long as it surpasses $500. If you need help, the Author Assist program costs $25, taken—if you succeed—from the total funds earned from supporters. Pubslush takes 4%, plus third-party processing fees. It also donates one children's book to a child in need for every book sold through their platform. Pubslush was founded in 2011 as a press (with crowdfunding), but its emphasis shifted to crowdfunding (with a press) in August 2012. It is the only platform that keeps your page up and links a "buy" button to your completed book for sale.

Pubslush author Janna Leyde was 14 years old when her father was in an automobile accident, leaving him with traumatic brain injury. The event drastically shifted her idyllic childhood and became the seed for "He Never Liked Cake," the only memoir about TBI that tells the story from the child's perspective. She used Pubslush to raise money to publish and market the book. Her life as a yoga teacher and a freelance writer/blogger on topics ranging from health and wellness to yoga and brain injury feeds the theme of her second book, "Yoga for Brain Injury: Move, Feel, Think."

Penny Rosenwasser Raised $10,097 on IndieGoGo

IndieGoGo was founded in 2007 as a place where people who want to raise money can create fundraising campaigns to tell their story and get the word out. It charges 4% of the money you raise if you meet your goal or 9% if you do not.

Penny Rosenwasser reached her $7,500 goal in eight days, enabling her take her self-published book "Hope into Practice: Jewish Women Choosing Justice Despite Our Fears," on the road.

A self-described rabble-rouser for justice, activist and author of two previous books, Rosenwasser is also a former performing folk musician, KPFA radio host/producer, women's music networker, festival organizer and diversity workshop leader. She is former Jewish Caucus Chair of the National Women's Studies Association and a founding board member of Jewish Voice for Peace. She teaches an Anti-Semitism/Anti-Arabism class with a Palestinian colleague at the City College of San Francisco.

Publisher-Assisted Crowdfunding

There are also two notable publisher-assisted platforms, Inkshares (based in San Francisco) and Unbound (in London). In return for taking on the task of raising money, editing, design, and distribution, they publish the book with a limited-time contract. They work with the author to create the crowdfunding campaign and, as InkShares specifies, "provide the tools to help you build a community of patrons, supporters, funders, collaborators and peers," and supply editing, design and manufacturing services. Here are InkShares' terms. I provide them to give you an idea of what fair terms look like.

> When you use our platform, we designate a funding floor. This is the amount necessary to cover the costs of editorial, design, and production of the first 1,000 print units. Once funds raised meet this amount, all subsequent book sales are considered orders. Inkshares will share gross revenue from these sales with you on a fifty-fifty split. Gross revenue is the price at which we sell your book. For example, if the retail price of your print book is $20.00 and is sold on Inkshares.com for $20.00, we pay you $10.00. Or, if we sell your print book for $10.00 to a bookstore through our distributor, we pay you $5.00. Print books funded by Inkshares. Inkshares may, at its discretion, choose to fund the production of print units. In the case that Inkshares, rather than the crowd, funds the production of a print unit, you receive 50% of gross revenue.
>
> *Print books funded by Inkshares.* Inkshares may, at its discretion, choose to fund the production of print units. In the case that Inkshares, rather than the crowd, funds the production of a print unit, you receive 50% of gross revenue.
>
> *Digital.* Inkshares shares revenues from digital sales with you on a seventy-thirty split, with seventy percent for you, the author, and thirty percent for us, Inkshares. The seventy-thirty split is based on gross revenue. For example, if Inkshares sells your ebook for $10.00 on Inkshares.com, you will be paid $7.00. Likewise, if we sell your ebook to Amazon.com for $6.00, Inkshares will pay you $4.20.

Your sales strategy

Your bookselling journey may be a short one, or it might be a long, fluid, and creative process. It can sometimes take years for a book to take off, so set up good channels, good relationships, and good communities. Never stop marketing. There are many ways to sell.

POD sales: By printing and distributing with a POD service such as CreateSpace, BookBaby or IngramSpark your print book is mailed to customers on-demand when they order from online retailers in their expanded distribution program.

Ebook sales: Create and sell ebooks in many formats for many ebook readers, for sales and distribution in the widest possible array of online markets. You can upload your ebook to each online retailer or outsource it to a company like Smashwords, KDP, BookBaby, or IngramSpark.

Direct: Use your website for direct sales in your own online store for both print and digital books. You can sell using PayPal, eJunkie, Gumroad, Selz or using any number of integrated payment systems.

Mailing physical books: Books fit nicely in a free USPS Priority Mail envelope, and a stamp costs about $5. (You can charge the customer for shipping.) Customers will receive the book in two days, which makes them very happy, especially during the holidays, and especially if it's autographed. Do send your books priority or first-class mail. The drastically lower cost of media mail might be tempting, but it can take a very long time to deliver, and sometimes—especially during the holidays—your book is likely to arrive to the customer later than they want. It also may be damaged as media mail bangs around at the bottom of the pile.

Retail sales: Sell to brick-and-mortar booksellers and retailers in your niche. When you sell direct to retailers, you can negotiate their discount. 40 to 50% is standard. You will probably be asked to sell on consignment, which means you won't be paid until the books are sold.

Back-of-room sales: Take advantage of back-of-room sales at personal appearances to earn 100% of profits. At some events, you may be asked to pay a small percentage to the organization or tip a cashier.

Specialty distribution: It's also possible to sell through specialty distributors—for example, someone who travels to conferences and sells books for you. Expect to discount your book 50 to 55%.

Exclusive distribution: If you've written a book to boost your business you may want to offload sales and distribution to a company who specializes in these tasks. These kinds of companies only take on books they think they can sell, so you'll need to pitch them. They also take a lot of your profits, 65% and up. The most popular solution for indie authors with commercially viable projects is IPG's Small Press United (SPU). SPU was formed as a branch of IPG's distribution service for traditional publishers to serve self-publishers. All the authors I know who have used them like them a lot. You may also choose a specialty small press to serve as your distributor. The sooner in the book creation process you can contact them, the better. They may have valuable insights and advice on editing, design, and production.

Pricing your book

You may be tempted to calculate the price of your book based on what it cost to produce it. That doesn't work; you really need to price your book to compete in the marketplace. Ebook prices are all over the place, but are becoming standardized at 20% to 25% less than the least expensive print edition. $9.99 also seems to be a consumer-accepted price for ebooks.

Some marketers will tell you that to succeed you should price your first ebook at free and subsequent books at 99 cents or $1.99 or $2.99. This may work for authors in particular genres, but it is probably not a good model for business books, or books that are also available in print. Study your competition to see what the market will bear and price accordingly. Don't be afraid to experiment with pricing or offer discounts and freebies to your social media followers and newsletter subscribers.

Setting expectations

The defining fact about traditional distributors is that they vet their work, whereas POD author services companies will print and distribute almost anything. A traditional distributor will have opinions. Their reputation is on the line, and they want to work with like-minded independent publishers dedicated to your success. Consider them a partner.

Do not dismiss the fact that, whatever route you take, you are responsible for the marketing and promotion that will create buzz and sell your book. That is; you can't just send the books to your distributor and expect them to sell magically. It can take years for even a very good book to rise to the top. Persistence pays off.

The Bowker record and ISBNs

Even though reputable companies like IngramSpark and BookBaby will handle your relationship with Bowker, assigning you a "portable" ISBN so that you can change vendors at will, I always think it's a better idea to own your own so that you can log in to your Bowker account and manipulate the metadata as you wish.

Don't make the mistake of allowing a company to assign one of their ISBNs to your book. As a professional indie publisher, you should be the publisher of record. When you own the relationship with Bowker, that is, when you register an account and buy ISBNs under your own publishing name, you control the book data. You can change the metadata, replace one book with another (that is, note that a book is retired and point the industry databases to the 2nd edition), and provide many other details to sales channels.

You can buy "portable" ISBNs from companies like BookBaby and CreateSpace, and if you're truly budget-strapped, go ahead. But it's a poor second.

So what if you've already bought a CreateSpace or an iUniverse ISBN and now you want your book to be free to distribute using, for example, IngramSpark? Unfortunately, your book is simply stuck with that ISBN and that company until you create a new edition using one of the ISBNs you own. To do this, discontinue distribution of your book with the service you used. Create a new edition with your own ISBN. In your Bowker record there's a place where you can record "replacement ISBN. Here's a screen shot of the Bowker record for this 3rd edition of my book, which replaces the ISBN for the 2nd edition book.

YOUR PUBLISHING BUSINESS

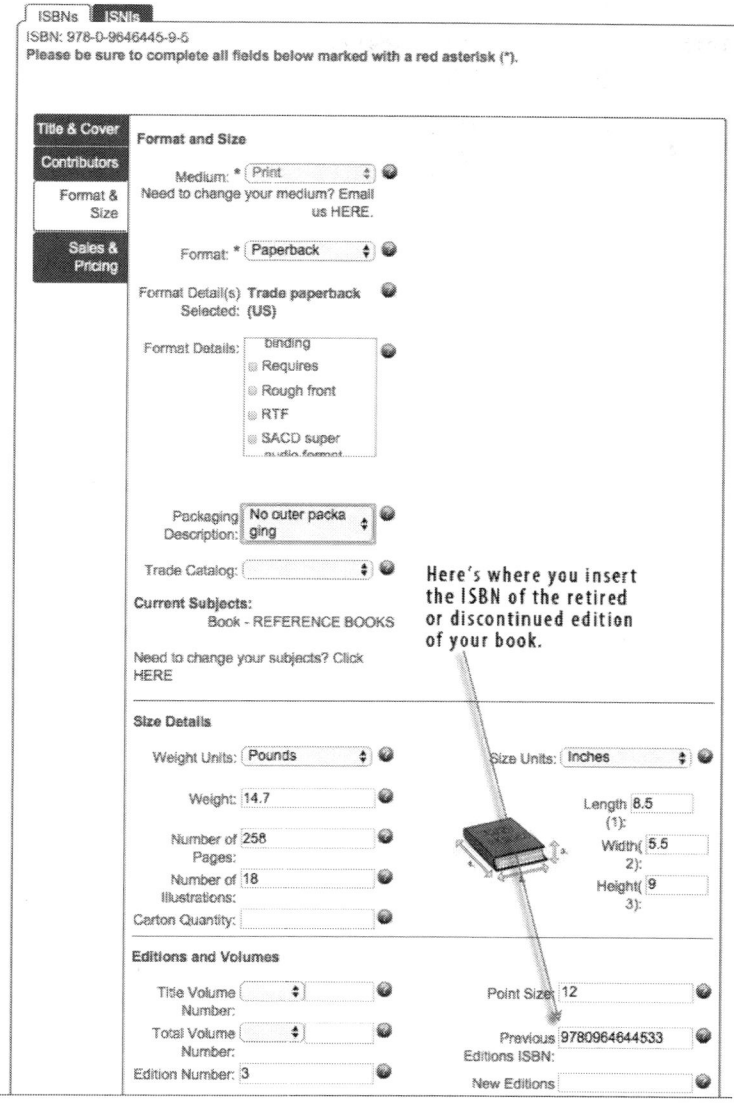

How to tell the world that your new edition replaces the old book. It may take a while for search engines to catch up.

Unfortunately, for a while, customers will only see that it is no longer available.

I don't know how I can hammer this point in any harder! Start out by buying your own ISBNs so you can distribute and print it with any company you like, without an interruption of service.

For more on Bowker and ISBNs see the chapter on metadata and discovery.

Registering your copyright

With the perceived risk among writers of copyright infringement so extremely high, it's no wonder authors are increasingly concerned about making sure their work is copyrighted.

Many self-publishing service companies now offer copyright services, but you don't need to use them. While they charge up to $150 for the service, it costs only $35 to easily do it yourself.

In reality, though, you might not need to register a copyright. U.S. copyright law states that copyright exists from the moment the work is created, "without any action taken by the author, the moment it is fixed in a tangible form so that it is perceptible either directly or with the aid of a machine or device."

You don't even have to put a copyright notice on your work, though it does ward off potential word thieves. You will have to register, however if you wish to bring a lawsuit for infringement.

One good reason to register copyright for your book is that acquisitions librarians scan recently copyrighted books to see if they might want to buy them. Since most self-publishers are not eligible to obtain a Library of Congress CIP record (you must be a small press who publishes three or more titles by different authors each year) this is a decent compromise. (See more about how to solve this problem in the section below on getting into libraries.)

So, go ahead and register for $35, in about 35 steps, as it so happens and, coincidentally, it took me about 35 minutes, too. See my PBS MediaShift post for a detailed step-by-step with screen shots. You'll see from the first screen on the US Government Copyright Registration page that they provide very detailed instructions. Do take a look at my post before you start so you can prepare all your materials and gather your information. There's a lot of it!

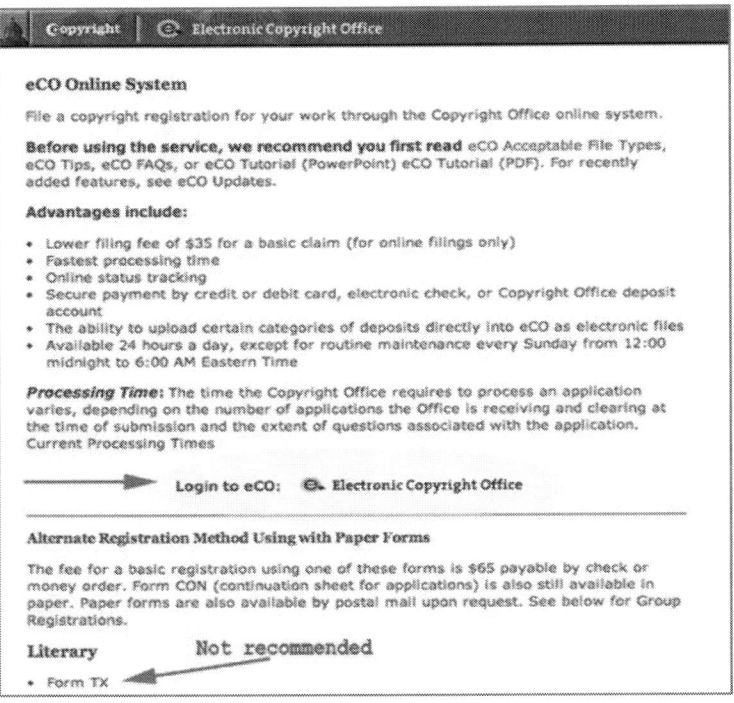

Filing copyright for your book in the USA.

You should receive a confirmation of your copyright in about four months. Each country has its own copyright office and the process is similar.

Getting into libraries

It's been difficult for self-publishers to get their print books into the library market and it may not be worth trying. I've suggested to many authors that they analyze the reality of the importance of the library market for their book before struggling with this step. About 90% of authors come to realize that it isn't the best place to focus their attention. It's no wonder. Acquisitions librarians are understandably overwhelmed, with approximately 300,000 titles by traditional publishers released each year and independent publishers releasing at least 100,000 more than that.

The self-publishing services industry is also trying very hard to solve the problem of getting indies into libraries. Smashwords has aggressively pursued the library market and has succeeded in getting many indie titles noticed. A book review in Kirkus, Library Journal, Publishers Weekly and the like will get it noticed. (Find more on book reviews in the chapter on marketing.)

A book review in Kirkus, Library Journal, Publishers Weekly and the like will get your book noticed by librarians, which may be a reason to pay for one. (Find more on book reviews in the chapter on marketing and promotion.) Join IBPA and participate in their

Another way to get in front of librarians is to join IBPA (Independent Book Publishers Association), and participate in their library mailing programs.

I have to mention CreateSpace because a lot of authors tell me they considered using one of their ISBNs because it makes their book available to libraries. There are many good reasons to use CreateSpace (to get your print book into Amazon; to print advance copies and drafts), but, as I have previously stated, using another company's ISBN is never advisable. Read on for better solutions.

Here's what you need to know about the library system.

- Library of Congress CIP number
- Library of Congress PCN program
- Local libraries
- Ebooks to libraries

Library of Congress CIP number

The Library of Congress website very plainly states that they do not allow self-publishers to obtain a number. You must be a small press, publishing books by at least three different authors. So how do you get around this? By applying to the PCN program.

Library of Congress PCN program

You may be able to get into the Library of Congress's Preassigned Control Number program "to obtain control numbers for your forthcoming books." Here's what the Library of Congress has to say about the difference between the CIP and PCN programs:

The Cataloging in Publication (CIP) program creates bibliographic records for forthcoming books most likely to be widely acquired by U.S. libraries. The Preassigned Control Number (PCN) program assigns a Library of Congress Control Number to titles most likely to be acquired by the Library of Congress as well as some other categories of books. The two programs are mutually exclusive.

The purpose of the Preassigned Control Number (PCN) program is to enable the Library of Congress to assign control numbers in advance of publication to those titles that may be added to the Library's collections.

Here are the requirements:

- The PCN program is for print books (not ebooks) in the U.S. only. (Smashwords can get your book into the ebook library market.)

- You must list a U.S. place of publication on the title or copyright page.

- You must obtain a block of 10 or more ISBNs from Bowker, assigned to your publishing house. During the application process, you'll need to enter your publisher identifier number (the third part of your ISBN).

- Apply online, and a few weeks later you should receive approval and your login credentials.

Local Libraries

If you want to market to a particular library or to libraries in a particular region, you should contact them directly. The Library of Congress website even advises working with your local librarian to obtain cataloging for your book. This is not limited to books considered local.

Your local librarian can help you get into the national library market.

A number of my self-publishing friends have done readings and spoken at library events, which are free but serve to expand their readership. Not to mention, make friends with the librarians, who will be that much more motivated to help you get noticed by other libraries.

Copyright

Copyrighting your book may also work to get you into libraries because acquisitions librarians scour the list of new copyrighted material quarterly. (Granted, there are more books than ever, so I don't imagine this is the best way to get attention.) I described how to copyright your book earlier in this chapter.

Ebooks to Libraries

I don't know about you, but I devour ebooks, and mostly I check them out for free on my local library website. How do self-publishers get into this market? By publishing your ebook with Smashwords, by using the same distributor as for your print book, or by using a new serviced called SELF-e.

Smashwords and Overdrive

In 2014, Smashwords announced an agreement to supply more than 200,000 titles to OverDrive, the world's largest library ebook platform. OverDrive powers the ebook procurement and checkout systems for 20,000 public libraries around the world, including to 90% of US public libraries. In their announcement, Smashwords had this encouraging news.

> *At a time when many large publishers are charging libraries high prices for ebooks (front list ebooks from Big 5 publishers can cost libraries $80, and even backlist ebooks can cost libraries $20-40), Smashwords authors and publishers are stepping in to supply thousands of affordably priced, library-friendly ebooks. Faced with the option of purchasing a single James Patterson novel for around $40.00, or ten thrillers from today's most popular indie authors at $4.00 each, libraries now have exciting new options to build patron-pleasing ebook collections.*

Smashwords also provided some additional stats to encourage you:

- Library patrons borrowed more than 102 million digital titles across the OverDrive network in 2013, up 44% over 2012.

- OverDrive delivered over 1.8 billion cover image impressions to library patrons in 2013, up almost 70% from 2012. This gives authors incredible exposure and branding to readers searching for their next read.

Using the same distributor as for print

Still, libraries are a hard market to tap. They pay attention to book reviews (see more on reviews in the marketing chapter), but since ebooks don't get reviewed, you might want to use the same distributor for your print and ebook. That way, the review pertains to both format. IngramSpark and BookBaby are two great options for both print and ebook distribution.

SELF-e

SELF-e is a collaboration between *Library Journal* and a company called BiblioBoard. If accepted, your book will be included in a "module" with other books made available to libraries from time to time. From the website:

Authors whose ebooks are selected by Library Journal for inclusion in our SELF-e modules can use a digital badge promoting their inclusion to potential readers who may choose to purchase a copy of the title and/or to purchase other books by that author via retail channels. Ebooks that are not selected by Library Journal will still be accessible to local library patrons via state-specific modules.

There's no cost to participate, and you make no money. So why would you use SELF-e? They claim that, "SELF-e is a marketing and discovery service aimed at helping authors build an audience of readers" So, if you've got a book with a message, and you want to get the word out, this will help. Or you can make it part of your marketing strategy. Find out more about SELF-e on their site. ♥

Self-Pub Boot Camp virtual workshop presentations that focus on doing business as an author include those by Helen Sedwick, author of the *Self-Publishers Legal Handbook* on *Setting Up Your Self-Publishing Business* and Karl Palachuk of Great Little Book Company on *Making Your Publishing Business a Business and Not a Hobby*. Find details on the Self-Pub Boot Camp virtual workshops and a complete list of resources at www.SelfPubBootCamp.com/resources.

CHAPTER FIVE

YOUR AUTHOR BRAND

Now's the time to start creating your public persona, including identifying images, graphics, words, and photographs that work in harmony with your author voice. Actually, the ideal time to start is years in advance, but it's never too late to begin. Here is a path to developing your author brand.

- Understanding brand
- Elements of your brand
- Your author bio
- Your author photo

Understanding brand

Your author brand is a big part of your author platform. It defines the way people perceive you in the marketplace. While brand may not be as important to you as it is to Dove soap or Nike, it warrants conscious consideration. Most authors don't think of brand at all, but creating and leveraging your brand can help you market yourself and your books.

For authors, when we talk about brand we're mostly talking about "voice." Each of us offers a unique experience to readers. But the emotional experience you deliver to readers can also be applied to visuals like your author photo, book covers, and website.

First tip: Create a plain, simple website rather than rushing through a poorly designed, ad-hoc site with clashing and confusing colors, typography and images. Try to build a consistent and recognizable presence, and keep at it for long enough that people start to recognize you.

I like Isabel Allende's website. It's simple and it features her, and only her. She can get away with this because she's so famous. Or maybe her webmaster (or PR firm), who's obviously really really good, and has worked with a marketing pro, or is a marketing pro, has decided that this is a trend for author websites. People do, after all, connect with people.

Isabel Allende's current website features the author above anything else. Well, Isabel does have "star author" status.

I liked Allende's old website, too. It definitely conveyed more information about her books, but it also managed to give you a hint about her as a person and a writer and the reading experience you were likely to find.

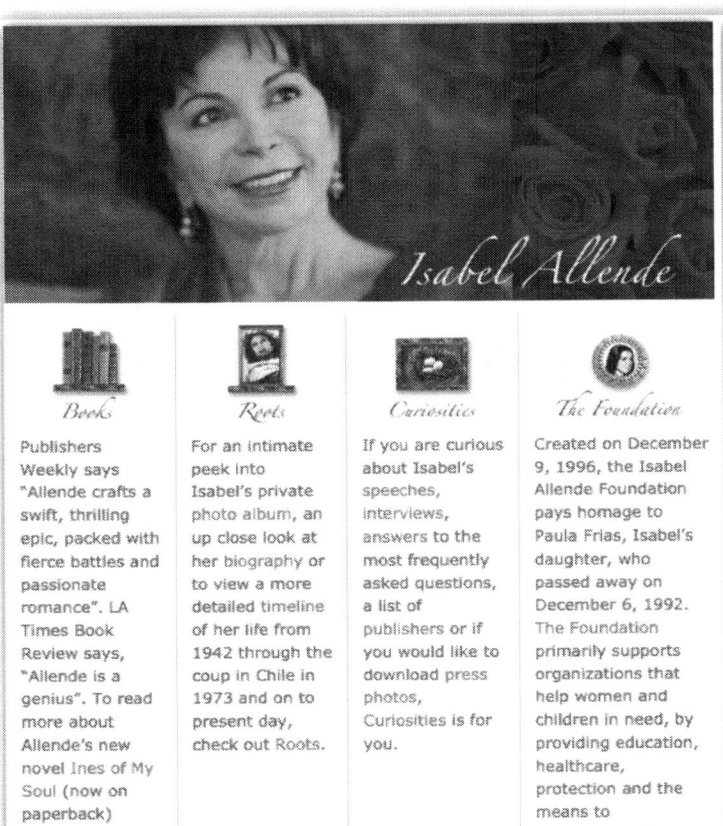

Isabel Allende's old website conveys a lot of information about her books and activities.

Why am I not discussing all this in the section on websites and blogs? I used to work in the San Francisco Bay Area as a web consultant, so the technical aspects of websites and writing for the web is very easy for geeks like me. But brand is subjective and elusive and it appears everywhere. It appears in your writing, on your website, your book covers and even your hair and your clothes, your house and the car you drive. I struggle with brand—with my adventure travel writer persona versus my self-publishing geek persona. Which one is me? Well, that's why I have two websites. Brand is style and, like many authors, I find that I cannot reconcile the two in one place.

Here is an attempt to nail the visual and style aspects of brand down into manageable chunks that you can use consistently so that readers can recognize you.

Your brand is made up of solid and recognizable trademark items like your author name, publisher or company name, photography, logo, colors, images, even typography.

In your author photo, elements of your brand might be considered personal style: a feather boa, a motorcycle, a hat, red lipstick, tweed jacket, your cat.

Brand is communicated on your website, social media profiles, stationery, posters, and other print materials.

Brand creates the feeling people have about you—the thing that you are known for. This is also called author platform.

Brand is reflected in your writing style, your media personality, your expertise or niche, and your overall image as reflected by your activities in person and in social media.

Elements of your brand

To organize elements of your brand you might want to create a brand worksheet or idea folder on your computer to collect images of visual brands that attract you. To save web pages, print to PDF and save them to your brand idea folder. Professional designers love getting this kind of input. It saves them from having to try to read your mind and thus costs you less in logo, website, and even book cover design.

- Web pages
- Book cover
- Company logo
- Graphics
- Author photos
- Color scheme
- Typography

The first thing you might want to do is to decide on your publishing house name. Choose a version of your name or something more descriptive. For example, I opted for Misadventures Media instead of choosing King Press or King Media.

But remember that your author name is your strongest brand. Decide on your author name or pen name and try to grab it for your domain name. Luckily I was able to buy CarlaKing.com early on. But if someone else with your name has already claimed yours, you may need to use your middle initial or incorporate the word "author" in your domain name.

A logo is an essential element of your media presence. Use it long enough and people will begin to recognize and trust it. It is important to develop a logo that is simple and effective in various sizes. It should look great both in color and grayscale. Your logo might incorporate your company (publishing house) name, or it may be a standalone graphic or type treatment.

Take a look at the spine and title pages of books at a library or bookstore and note which publisher logos are effective and why. Sketch out some ideas for your logo and collect examples of logos you like before contacting a designer. You can find people to create a logo fairly inexpensively by using a crowdsourcing site like 99 Designs or even Fiverr. You might also look for a book design professional on a site like Writer.ly, Bibliocrunch, or Reedsy. Remember that, though you could get lucky, you often get what you pay for.

Your author bio

Your biographical description is an extremely important asset that affirms your author brand. Information you share about yourself may include your education, accomplishments, professional qualifications, awards, titles, prior publications, media appearances, location, and family information.

If you're writing an academic book you know that your education and awards need to be highlighted. Business book authors must point to their expertise. Authors of historical fiction will be taken more seriously if there is a clear connection to place and time. If you write fiction, romance or children's books, take a look at authors that compete in your particular genre and follow the lead of the most successful authors.

Like an elevator speech, your author bio should be entertaining, informative, not dry and boring. It also needs to convey how you are uniquely qualified, talented, or fascinating enough that anyone will want to read your book.

Author bios can be used on the back of the book, your website, on other people's websites, in press and news releases, in magazine articles, advertisements, speeches, at dinners, and as introductions by interviewers. A good test is to read it out loud, just like the host of a radio show would, and gauge whether the listener would change the channel or stay tuned.

Create several different bios to apply to different media, from long to short: between 30 and 250 words for various websites and social media, and just 140 characters for Twitter. Write your bio in the appropriate tone. Consider a tag line or a title. Also make sure your bios are keyword-rich, so search engines can help you market (as explained in the chapter on discovery).

In my workshops I like to divide authors into groups of three people who don't know each other. Each author is interviewed by the other two for five minutes. Those two people then write the bio of the author interviewed. Then we switch, and everybody gets two bios to use as source material for their author bio. It works because most of us are too shy to brag about our accomplishments and besides, it's difficult to know what's interesting about ourselves. Lots of great bios have come out of these exercises. Maybe you can find two strangers who are authors to share this exercise with you. And, who knows, that may be the beginning of a writing group.

Your author photo

Your photo is a recognizable part of your author brand, so make sure that it is fairly recent, or at least really does still look like you. It should sharply frame your head and neck and look good in both color and grayscale.

Do try to avoid shots with a lot of competing activity in the background, or one where you've Photoshopped out your ex. You will need to be clearly recognized, even when the photo is reduced to the size of a postage stamp, because that's about all the space some social media sites give you.

Decide what you want to convey to readers about you in your author headshot—studiously sexy, geeky glam, adventurous, goofy, beautiful, serious or shy. Also write down the physical qualities you want to highlight—your hair, eyes, or smile. What look will attract your audience? Trustworthy (or untrustworthy)? Exciting and smart and funny? Entrepreneurial bohemian? You get the picture.

How do you hire a good photographer? Well, it probably should not be that gal at the drugstore who snapped your passport photo. Maybe you're lucky enough to have a talented photographer in your circle of friends or family. You may find one at a writer's conference. (A smart local photographer snaps authors photos at the San Francisco Writers Conference for $50. Which is a great deal.)

Look for portrait photographers in your area. You see them all over the place, parading families into scenic settings, coaxing smiles from cranky toddlers. Expect to pay between $50 and $200 for a session depending on how much time they spend with you in various settings, plus an order minimum.

Yes, all this does cost money and is included in my outline of budget basics in the chapter on doing business as an author. Remember, indie authors (that's you!) are businesspeople in the publishing industry, and budgets and financial planning are critical to success. ♥

Self-Pub Boot Camp virtual workshop presentations that highlight brand and platform include those by Brian Felsen, founder of BookBaby on *Social Media and Branding Essentials*, Penny Sansevieri, founder of Author Marketing Experts, and Nina Amir with her presentation on *How to Write a Short Book Fast*. Find details on the Self-Pub Boot Camp virtual workshops and a complete list of resources at www.SelfPubBootCamp.com/resources.

CHAPTER SIX

WEBSITES & BLOGS

Your website is a storefront and a scrapbook, a place to attract, inform, connect, collect, and communicate. Your website is "You-Central." But the most important function of your website is to win a personal connection with readers by getting them to hand over their email address. When they give you their email address, they have given you permission to contact them directly. So whatever you put on your web pages, make sure to place your email news signup form at the top right of your site because this is where people expect it to be. Website visitors are tired of being sold to, so entice them with an "ethical bribe." This could be a free story, tip sheet, or anything you can think of that has informational or entertainment value to your audience. (I use MailChimp's email marketing service.)

Use static pages and blog posts to make your site compelling and useful. It's not important that readers come back to your website as long as they give you that email address! You can also entice them to connect with you where they spend the most time, in their social stream, whether it be Facebook, Twitter or Pinterest.

With the most important stuff out of the way, here's all the technical stuff you need to know to take the mystery out of creating a website and blog.

- Choosing a domain name
- Choosing web hosting
- Building your website
- Setting up your blog
- Widgets and social media links

Choosing a domain name

Your domain name is an important part of your brand, so consider it carefully. You should not only buy your name (and your pen name and nicknames), but the name of your book and the name of your publishing house. You can "redirect" or "forward" all those domain names to your main website, which is, ideally, your author name.

If your name is difficult to spell, try to buy the common misspellings as well, and forward those domains to your main site. If you have a common name, it is likely to be taken. If not, grab it now and choose .com—don't bother with .net and .org or .biz or .tv or any of the other tags if you can get a .com tag. If you cannot get a .com tag for your author name, consider adding your middle initial (carlasking.com), or use a dash or underscore (carla-king.com or carla_king.com) or even append the word "author" or "writer" to your name (such as carlaking-author.com). If you write for a niche market, you might use a descriptive word in your name (carlaking-motorcycles.com) and if you have a great nickname, use it (missadventuring.com).

Here are some tips for selecting and managing domain names:

- Write down all the domain names you might need, and search for their availability.

- Buy them. GoDaddy sells domain names cheaply and offers bulk discounts. They also offer managed WordPress hosting and an email service. It's great to have everything in one place.

- Set your main website to renew automatically so you don't lose your domain name when it expires.

- Buy your most important domain names for the maximum number of years possible instead of 1 or 5 years. Search engines give more weight to domains that have really committed.

- Redirect, or forward, all the names you buy to your main website.

Choosing web hosting

When you're first deciding on creating or redesigning your website, you'll probably be overwhelmed. Most authors use WordPress. Others use SquareSpace, Wix, or Weebly.

My best recommendation for creating new websites is to use GoDaddy's managed WordPress hosting.

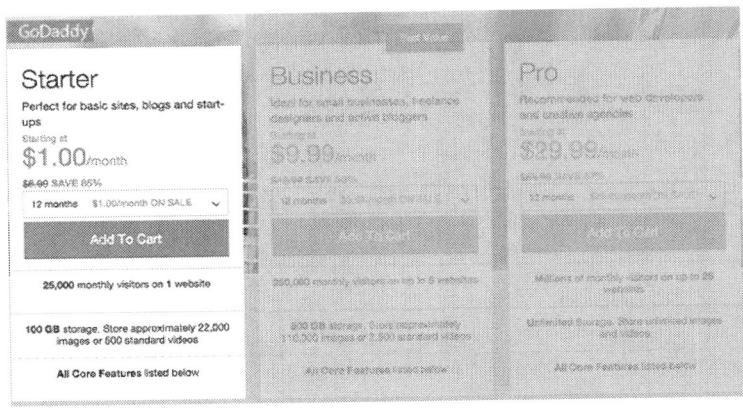

GoDaddy Managed Wordpress Hosting is my recommendation for safe, reliable and inexpensive web hosting.

As a professional author-publisher, you need a self-hosted website and not a blog-based website that has the name of the blogging company in the URL. For example, carlaking.com is great but carlaking.wordpress.com is not so good. Neither is carlaking.blogger.com, or a typepad or squarespace or wix address. Always remember that your name is your strongest brand, so don't dilute it with a brand that doesn't belong to you.

Other website builders include Wix and Weebly, both of which are very easy to use. If you want a really polished visual website, Wix does a good job but you might like Squarespace better.

If you're selling your books on your own site, the best choices are Squarespace, Weebly and Jimdo with built-in ecommerce. WordPress plugins also easily allow you to do commerce on your WordPress site (selling books and other things), as well as the ability to plug in widgets from Gumroad, Selz, and eJunkie.

I really like WordPress best. One reason I like it is because so many people know how to use it, so I know that I can hire anyone anytime at relatively little cost to help me handle the things I struggle with. WordPress easily lets you plug-in services like MailChimp for mailing list management and newsletters, Google Analytics for site statistics, Flickr for photos and so on.

But do some research to find a solution that's best for you. Here is a checklist of features to help you figure it out.

- **Editable web pages:** All site builders give you the ability to change the words and photos on your site whenever you like by logging in from any web browser.

- **Blog:** An integrated, fully featured blog should be incorporated, and WordPress is the standout product for this.

- **Reader reviews:** A form on the website lets readers type in a review of your book or product. You get notification and can edit and publish the review (or not). WordPress and other site builders let you create forms.

- **Contact form:** A contact form on your website allows readers and press to directly contact you from the site. This means that you don't have to publish your email address.

- **Mailing list management and newsletter tool:** I like MailChimp but also popular are AWeber, Constant Contact, and Vertical Response. There are many others. Readers sign up for your mailing list via a form. Bounces and bad email addresses are removed automatically. Include the URL for mailing list signup on all of your correspondence, and watch your list grow. Make sure your newsletter is branded consistently with your website. You may have multiple mailing lists, such as one for readers and one for the press, or any topic of your choice.

- **Store:** Add an integrated store (PayPal, eJunkie, Gumroad, Selz) for print and digital downloads. An integrated store keeps customers on your site, takes credit cards and automates shipping and tax calculations.

- **Search Engine Optimization (SEO):** Optimize your search engine placement by specifying keywords and other metadata. Search the WordPress plugins direction for popular solutions.

- **Multimedia:** Upload photos, create albums, slideshows, audio, and video.

- **Site statistics:** Monitor site popularity and marketing campaign success with website statistics reports that detail users, referrers, visitor locations and more. Make sure to install Google Analytics so you know where people have come from, what pages they're visiting, how long they're staying and things like that.

- **Social media features:** Place widgets on your site that display your activities on Twitter, Facebook, Scribd and other sites, making sure not to detract readers from signing up for your email newsletter or buying your book.

Social media widgets and buttons help your readers find you in their favorite places.

It might be difficult to decide on a method and service to use to develop and maintain your website. But here are some questions to ask yourself:

- Do you have a webmaster that you trust to keep your site updated as you evolve?
- Do you want to do it yourself using tools provided by your ISP? (GoDaddy, for example.)
- Maybe you prefer an all-in-one browser-based CMS (HostBaby or Yola).

In my opinion, the best option by far is a hosted WordPress site and blog.

With this information you should be able to research and decide on a system you can use. Browse and evaluate other author websites to gauge their effectiveness and get ideas. Use VIEW > SOURCE to find out what website system they're using.

Building your website

Just like a house, a website should be built with a solid and proven foundation and architecture. Web professionals who structure large sites for corporations are actually called information architects. But your site needn't be complex. You can easily build a basic site and add on later. Here are some standard foundational pages you might start with.

HOME | ABOUT | BLOG | BOOKS | REVIEWS | MEDIA | CONTACT

Many authors nest the MEDIA in a subheading under ABOUT, and the REVIEWS page under BOOKS. Do use the word "books" instead of "book." That way when you write another book you won't have to change the name of the page, and hard links to your BOOKS page won't be broken.

Now a word about creativity. I've seen many authors, tiring of these standard headings, getting creative with their page titles. As much as we love being creative writers, please resist the urge to get cute with headings. Visitors become quickly impatient and will click away immediately if they cannot find the pages they want. These headings may seem boring to you but, as standards, they are effective.

Here is a checklist for creating content for your website:

Home: You really need to hook your readers on this page. Use great copywriting and a free giveaway to make it irresistible to sign up for your free email newsletter.

Once you've got their email you can woo them into buying your books without a hard sell. Read more on email newsletters in the chapter on marketing and promotion.

About: Include a generous bio with an author headshot. The ABOUT page is the most visited page on any site. Don't be shy. You're wrong if you believe people shouldn't be interested in you. They are. Remember, no matter how great your book is, people connect with people. So be a human.

Media: Include a good media page that journalists, bloggers and interviewers can use as backgrounders. Make sure you provide them with a collection of bios of various word counts that media people can choose from, along with very high quality versions of your author headshot, book covers and other photos appropriate to interviews and articles. Also include details about your book—those boring bits like ISBNs and publication dates, along with the standard book description and any other information you think media may be interested in using. Joel Friedlander has a great media kit template for author websites.

Store: Whether you use PayPal, Gumroad, Aerbook, eJunkie, Selz or any other system, make sure your readers can easily buy your book. Yes, go ahead and point them to Smashwords, Amazon, B&N, Kobo, and the other resellers but, if possible, also make it easy to buy direct from you. (Especially those super-cool personalized autographed print editions.)

Make sure that readers have the ability to share your content on social media by providing sharable content they can easily post on Facebook, Scribd, Twitter, Pinterest, and other sites.

Reviews: Add any reader reviews to this page, and clip reviews from Amazon and bloggers with links to those sites.

Contact: Make it easy for authors to contact you using a form on your site so you don't have to publish your email address. By the way, your email address should be your domain name, not Gmail, Yahoo, Comcast and such. Mine, for example, is carla@carlaking.com. This is easy to set up in GoDaddy and other web hosting sites. Email services also provide premium services that let you do this.

Blog... well, that's a big subject. There is plenty of great advice for authors from professionals on developing content for your blog, but it is all incredibly subjective. I am just going to give you the basic on how to set one up.

Setting up your blog

The most popular blogging tool today by far is WordPress, which has evolved into an extremely popular website builder. So you can have a WordPress website and a blog all in the same package. But even if your weblog is not integrated with your website, you can display your blog feed on your site by including an RSS feed. That may be something you pay a web professional to do. Here are the steps to getting your blog set up.

Choose a blog tool that suits you. (WordPress has become the defacto tool for author blogs, though content management systems like HostBaby have great blog tools, too and I've already also mentioned SquareSpace and many other site builders, which also incorporate blogging systems.)

Set up your account. Be sure to upload your author photo and bio, fill out your profile information using good keywords (see the chapter on metadata and discovery).

Publish an introduction to yourself, a short description of what you expect to be blogging about, and how often.

Create an RSS feed to your blog so that people can subscribe. (I like Feedburner.) Make sure the RSS feed is in addition to your email newsletter signup form, and not instead of your email newsletter.

Every time you blog, send out the link on Twitter, Facebook, Pinterest and other social media sites to let people know that you've posted a new entry. (Find out more about social media marketing in the next chapter.)

Widgets and social media links

You can embed widgets and social media links into your website and blog so that people can join your communities and even preview your book. These are great marketing tools that can grow your platform enormously. Here are just a few examples.

Twitter

Use Twitter's widget to display your Twitter updates on any webpage, or any number of other widgets. Below is Twitters widget creation tool.

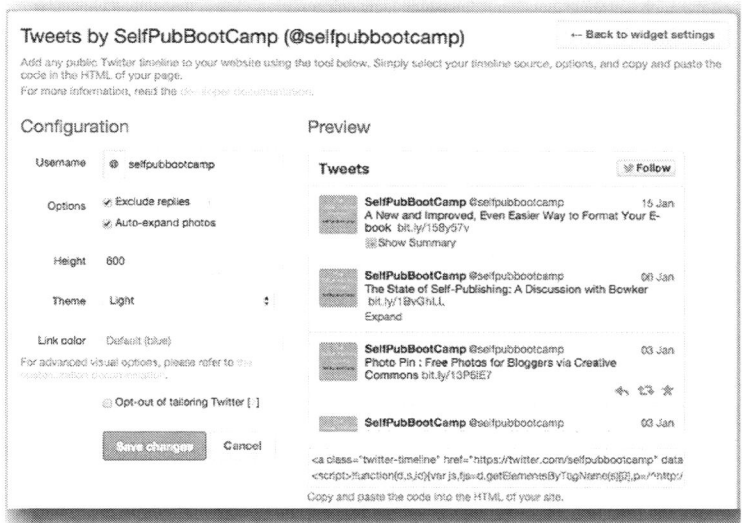

Twitter and the other social media platforms make it super easy to create a widget to embed in your website.

Facebook

Especially useful for authors is the Facebook "Like" button, which lets people share pages from your site back to their Facebook profile with one click. The Comments plugin lets users comment on any piece of content on your site. The Activity Feed plugin shows users what their friends are doing on your site through likes and comments. There's a huge number of Facebook widgets, buttons and badges, available from the Facebook and WordPress sites, among others.

WordPress Widgets for Flicker, Goodreads, etc.

Here are a few examples of WordPress widgets that you can include on your WordPress website or blog.

- The Flickr widget lets you display thumbnails of your latest Flickr photos in your sidebar.

- The Goodreads widget lets you feature some of the books you've listed on your reading list there.

- The Follow Blog widget enables your readers to sign up to receive your WordPress blog posts via email.

- The RSS widget displays posts from any RSS feed. You might find this handy if you want to show off one of your other blogs, or one of your favorite blogs, in your sidebar.

- The Twitter widget allows you to display a Twitter feed in your WordPress blog's sidebar.

WEBSITES AND BLOGS

Document Sharing Widgets

One of my favorite document sharing sites is Scribd, with their ability to embed your documents into virtually any web page or blog. When you embed a document on your web page, it'll appear inside their document viewer right inside that page. For example, you can publish a sample chapter of your book on Scribd, place the widget for that document on one of your web pages or blog posts, and people can read it inside the Scribd viewer directly on your web page without needing to download anything or even visit the Scribd.com website.

The SlideShare Playlist widget lets you embed a custom playlist of presentations and documents on your blog or website. You can choose a feed from your tags, groups or events, or from your uploaded or favorited SlideShare content.

YouTube

If you post a lot of videos to YouTube, embed a subscribe widget on your site. Get the HTML code by searching for "YouTube Widget." It looks something like this:

> *<iframe id="fr" src="http://www.youtube.com/subscribe_widget?p=[add YouTube Username here]" style="overflow: hidden; height: 105px; width: 300px; border: 0;" scrolling="no" frameBorder="0"><-/iframe>*

Overwhelmed? There are a lot of freelance WordPress experts. Get recommendations from author friends, organizations, and communities. ♥

The Self-Pub Boot Camp virtual workshop features WordPress expert Linda Lee on *Building Your Wordpress Blog and Website*, plus Nina Amir on *How and Why to Blog Your Book* and, in another session, *How to Write a Short Book Fast*. Find details on the Self-Pub Boot Camp virtual workshops and a complete list of resources at www.SelfPubBootCamp.com/resources.

CHAPTER SEVEN

MARKETING & PROMOTION

By now you're probably already overwhelmed and, ugh, it's time for a marketing talk! Don't worry, any marketing you can do is good marketing. It doesn't matter if you start late, just start. Marketing, like writing, is something that only you can do. It's very very difficult to hire it out, and very expensive. But marketing doesn't have to be painful. After all, you're marketing to your tribe, to people you want to hang out with, to people who are going to love your book. All you have to do is find them. Best yet, you don't even have to change out of your favorite sweatpants.

This chapter focuses on strategy and traditional marketing and promotion. Social media marketing is addressed the next chapter. The first thing I think you need to do is to take a breath and look at the mission and goals you created in your business plan. (See the chapter on your publishing business.) Oops! Didn't do it? Now's the time to set down your goals. Figure out what do you want to achieve. How much work you are willing to do to get there. How much time you have to spend on it. How much money.

Here are some ideas on how to market your book and yourself as an author. There are many more. In fact, there are entire books written about it. I hope this chapter will give you a good start.

- Your mailing list
- Hiring out publicity
- Your online press kit
- Press releases
- Book reviews
- Professional organizations
- Trade organizations
- Make your book discoverable
- Use Amazon's promotional tools

Your mailing list

Your email newsletter your most important marketing tool. It gives you direct access to readers who are interested in you, whether they've found your website or they've met you at a conference or read a story you wrote in a magazine.

MARKETING AND PROMOTION

You can get a free mailing list account with MailChimp for the first 2000 email addresses. They make it easy to place a signup form on your website and blog.

I think it's a bit funny that authors find it intimidating to write an email newsletter. After all, we are writers. On the other hand, marketing is a huge mental barrier. But you don't have to be a salesperson.

What do you say in an email newsletter? A welcome message, to start. A free tip sheet. A draft of a story. You can let them know about excerpts you've published on social publishing sites or a guest blog post you've written. Be generous and genuine. Here are some tips for marketing:

- Build a social media presence using a tool you're comfortable with. Just choose one and start. (I cover social media marketing in the next chapter.) You'll find one that you like, and it will boost discoverability to search engines and build your author platform by gaining readers, reviewers, and influencers.

- Don't be shy about contacting reporters in traditional media: podcast hosts, local news reporters, and even television news producers. They will call you if they need your expertise.

- Create a media page. (Guess what? Our friend Joel Friedlander offers a media kit for author websites.) Collect materials for your online press room for the media. Include high-resolution photos of you and your book covers.

- Include a signature block in your emails that include your book's name, website, and email newsletter sign-up page.

- Offer a free sample chapter to your followers, mailing list members, friends, and to readers of articles you publish.

- Use coupon codes. Create a different code for each market so that you can track the effectiveness of each venue. Smashwords offers coupon codes and so do other services.

- Use Bitly to shorten links so you can track who clicked on them. Analytics help you figure out what readers are actually interested in. Honestly, you'll be surprised.

- Contribute stories to as many print and online publications as you can, and include bio and book order information in lieu of payment. Marketing is expensive, and this is an inexpensive way to market effectively to a target audience.

- Create a news release each time news happens on your topic, to relate you and your book to current events.

- Participate in podcasts, or even start your own.

- Offer discounts or free shipping to social media friends and friends of friends.
- Create audio and video clips of your readings or an interview to post on your website and social media sites.
- Consider producing a book trailer to post on YouTube.

Here are some ideas for offline marketing tasks.

- Find Meetup groups in your region who want or need the information in your book, or start a group.
- Scan Help A Reporter Out (HARO) for media opportunities.
- Pay for a targeted media list when you're ready to send a press release.
- Send free copies of your book to podcasters, journalists, reviewers, interviewers and conference organizers. Make sure you know them and that they actually want your book. And do make sure that this is not the first time they've ever heard from you. Marketing is about relationships.

Hiring out publicity

For the indie author, affordable professional publicity is nearly impossible to find, and it's difficult to justify or measure the return on investment. The problem is that nobody can guarantee which publication, blog, radio, or TV show will run with a review of an author's book, or who will interview the author as an expert. Still, there are certain things a dedicated publicist can do to customize the PR campaign and improve the odds the writer will get picked up by media.

An alternative to a traditional publicist is a virtual assistant, who might help you set up, monitor and maintain your social media presence or draft blogs for you. (There's a list of author assistants in the resources section of this book.)

When interviewing someone to help you, request a detailed plan that includes the specific projects that will be part of the job, the timeline for delivering on these projects, what you as the author are expected to provide, and the process by which your helper will keep you updated on the progress of your campaign. And be sure to ask for references.

Here are some tips for hiring out publicity.

- Consider employing a virtual assistant or marketing pro.
- What do they charge? And for what, exactly? (Sending out news releases, blog tour setup, social media help, etc.)

- How do they go about it? Ask about their process and approach.

- What is their actual expertise and experience? Ask for a list and references.

- How well do you connect personally? Do you like each other?

- How personalized is the service?

Your online press kit

Your website is the centerpiece of your marketing effort, as I've described in the chapter on setting up your website. Your author brand, the topic of yet another chapter, is inextricably linked to marketing and your website. Make sure your website has a press or media page where reporters can easily get the materials they need for articles and interviews. They should be able to download high-resolution author photos and your book cover. You should also provide links to all the media that have interviewed you or published your articles and stories. Find a media kit for author websites in Joel Friedlander's collection of templates.

Press releases

Many press release distribution services promise distribution to national and international media outlets for less than $500, which sounds very attractive. But press releases have to be incredibly well-written, titillating, topical (automotive, gardening, etc.) or timely (tied to a major news event) to get noticed by busy journalists, and there's no guarantee it will be picked up.

Look for a service that will provide a targeted media list based on keywords, who will help you write a great press release, and provide you with a monthly newswire service. I pass on recommendations in my email newsletter.

Think creatively. You might hire a magazine editor or well-known personality in the field you're writing about to send emails to their contacts. The email can have all the information a press release has in it, but crafted as a personal note. For example, I hired a retired motorcycle magazine editor to send out an email to her peers about my new book on motorcycle travel. You can bet those editors clicked on her email when they would have completely ignored an email from me, an unknown, or a press service. As a result, news of my book was included in every major motorcycle magazine in the country, and it also reached a lot of the international publications.

Book reviews

There are many ways to get book reviews, including paying for reviews, a practice that was at first widely criticized but has become accepted. Perhaps that's because a paid review does not guarantee a good review. It's time to

MARKETING AND PROMOTION

think of paid review services as a necessity, the same as paying for editing, formatting, and design. It's just another service that self-publishers have at their disposal and it's desperately needed to gain attention in an evermore crowded book market. A paid review can be expeditious, which is an advantage if you're looking for reviews to include with launch materials. Expect reviews to take 6-9 weeks. Some services provide expedited services for an additional fee.

- Kirkus Reviews charges around $500, as does Clarion Reviews.

- The Independent Book Publishers Association's excellent NetGalley Book Review Program lets you pitch your book to bloggers and reviewers from one location for $399. (Get a deal on NetGalley if you're a member of IBPA.) Miral Satar of Bibliocrunch published a useful interview with NetGalley on how self-published authors can use the service.

- A review from San Francisco Book Reviews costs $125 ($299 for an expedited review). You don't need to live in the city to use the service.

- You can submit your book to unpaid book review sites like BookLife's PW Reviews, but it may be declined for review.

- Publishers Weekly offers PW Select ($149), which gets your book in the magazine and its websites,

- newsletter, social media channels, as well as a listing in its special announcements database, and subscriptions to its magazines.

- The Indie Reader offers reviews for $225. If your title earns 4 to 5 stars, it will be included in IR's Curation Services, which to date include Scribd (the ebook subscription service) and Bibliolabs (which works with libraries). They also recommend titles to the Huffington Post and USA Today.

- Blue Ink Review only reviews indie and self-published books ($395).

- BookRooster charges a very reasonable administrative fee of $67 to send your book to appropriate (unpaid) reviewers.

- Some avid readers have become book bloggers, taking the challenge to find and recommend great books. Find some of them at The Book Blogger List, a place to "help book bloggers find like-minded bloggers and help authors find book bloggers that might be interested in their book."

- LibraryThing connects authors with potential readers, and you may be able to find reviewers here with their book giveaway program.

- Register to see the list of book review bloggers on The IndieView. The list starts with "prolific indie reviewers."

- Author Assistant Kate Tilton provides a list of reviewers on her website.

Some reviewers post reviews on their blogs, others on Amazon and Goodreads. I was approached last year by a woman who wrote a book about a solo bicycling adventure in Italy on my Adventure Travel Books group on Goodreads. It was similar in topic and spirit to one of my books, which she said she had read. Her message to me was well-written, funny, and not at all pushy. It's important not to be pushy when approaching an author who is known in your genre. They get a lot of requests, and it can be burdensome. Yes, I read the book and reviewed it favorably.

Be creative! I was recently encouraging the author of a fictional book featuring Shakespeare to cultivate relationships with famous actors and directors of current Shakespeare plays. She already knows a few, as she teaches and directs students about the bard and his works, so she can test the waters by approaching them first. I advised her not to necessarily ask for reviews, but offer the book (digital or print edition), as a gift after a conversation or an email exchange or two. I think it's important not to burden a potential reviewer with an obligation to read the book, especially if you've never met the person before. They might even not like to read. But who knows? They may be very pleased and honored. Still, a too-quick request might also cause alienation and can kill the relationship before it starts.

Don't be afraid to use your social media connections, especially at LinkedIn, to cast about for reviewers from known names. After all, you already have a relationship with these folks.

Professional organizations

Many writers work in isolation and striking out into the larger community can provide you with an energizing boost. Plus, it is beneficial to your ongoing promotional needs to keep up with changes in the industry, new technologies, services and sales and distribution channels. Here are some communities you might consider.

- Independent Book Publishers Association (IPBA, formerly PMA—Publishers Marketing Association) is the biggie, and I highly recommend joining. They provide discounts on everything from ISBNs to printing. They also produce a print magazine (yes, print, delivered to your house), which is incredibly educational, and their annual conference is an amazing learning opportunity. There are many regional spinoffs. For example, I belong to Publishers and Writers San Diego as well as IBPA.

- Local publishers organizations and associations have the advantage of offering face-to-face meetings, opportunities, and commiseration. You may not need to be a member to attend their events. Search for "independent publishers associations" in your area.

- Meetup has lots of writing, reading and social groups for authors, not to mention groups in business or social niches. I run a Meetup group for self-publishers in San Diego.

Trade organizations

You might benefit from relationships with trade organizations related to your topic. Funded by dues, they have money and may host, sponsor, or organize conferences. They are often eager to enliven their program with an author appearance. Some examples of trade organizations are The Fragrance Foundation, Organic Trade Association, International Housewares Association, Motorcycle Industry Council, Adventure Travel Trade Association, and The United States Association of Professional Investigators. These are just a very few of the thousands of trade organizations that you might mine for publicity opportunities.

The value of contacts in trade organizations related to the topic of your book, or that your fictional character specializes in cannot be underestimated. They're large groups—a captive audience of people who want to hear more about what they do.

Make your book discoverable

With the decline of bookstores and the rise of the web, it is more and more important that your book be visible to search engines. Search Engine Optimization (SEO) is critical to your web strategy, and that includes getting the right metadata on the right pages.

It's also important that you have control of your book's data in the major book record keeping and discovery system, specifically Bowker My Identifiers, where you buy and manage ISBNs.

You'll need a gravatar (globally-recognized avatar, more on that later in the chapter on metadata and discovery), so that the web can track your comments and contributions and allow people to trace you to your website and biographical data.

These are just a few of the discoverability systems that, thanks to the internet, will help promote your book while you sleep. For details, see my chapter on metadata and discovery, a powerful passive marketing partner.

Amazon's promotional tools

Amazon likes to sell books, and they keep developing ways to sell more. This can be great for authors, and even though some of their promotional opportunities are exclusive, their programs can help to jump-start your book marketing efforts. They provide extensive how-to pages to make it easy to succeed with their programs.

Amazon Author Central

Author Central is your author home page in the world's biggest bookstore. Along with your bio, you can add multimedia, blog feeds, a Twitter feed and events. You can edit or correct Amazon's list of your books, claiming all your books, so they can be listed correctly on your bibliography. A Sales tab lets you track your book sales over time, you can check your current Amazon ranking, and all your reviews are collected on one page. Search for Author Central pages in various countries. I created a page for Canada, the UK, India, Australia, and various European countries, for those residents who can read in English.

Behind the scenes, you can look at sales data, make corrections to book data, link multiple editions, remove books, and even report copyright infringement, to name just a few functions.

These pages are popular with readers in the largest bookstore in the world, and lets them know what other books you've written and where to find you elsewhere on the web.

Kindle KDP Select

Your participation in the exclusive KDP Select program gives you access to Amazon Kindle marketing programs but you give up the ability to sell anywhere else, even your own website. You agree to sell your book exclusively for Kindle for 90 days in exchange for inclusion in the program. It will automatically renew for additional 90-day periods unless you opt out through the KDP website beforehand. Many authors make the mistake of just letting this go on and on forever. There are pros and cons to going exclusive, such as the inability to give away books or distribute to the major stores using Smashwords, BookBaby, IngramSpark, and others. So weigh them carefully. There is also the additional political view that Amazon's attempt with the exclusive program is to cut out "pure play" stores like B&N and Kobo. (Pure play meaning that stores, unlike Amazon and Apple, sell only books, not other products.) Many authors and readers want to keep pure play stores in business, so they boycott this program. I think it's interesting that this "save the stores" controversy has shifted from brick-and-mortar indie bookstores, which have all but died out, to these businesses.

Programs like the Kindle Owners Lending Library and Kindle Unlimited available to KDP Select authors earn paltry royalties. All the authors in the program share the

MARKETING AND PROMOTION

funds allotted for that time period. Amazon offers this example: "if the fund for a particular month is $500,000, your Digital Book is borrowed 1,500 times, and all participating Digital Books are cumulatively borrowed 100,000 times, your Digital Book will earn $7,500 ($500,000 x 1,500/100,000 = $7,500)." Unfortunately, Amazon does not reveal the amount of funds available until after the period ends.

I discourage these KDP-Select related "perks" for a few reasons. First, because you only earn a tiny fraction of what you would earn from selling in Smashwords, B&N, Kobo, Apple, and other stores. Second, because exclusivity prevents you from marketing and selling to readers who shop in other online retailers. Third, because Amazon uses Kindle Unlimited to avoid paying authors according to the industry standard Agency model (versus the Wholesale model). And finally, because Amazon is trying to squeeze out other online ebook retailers, and is doing a pretty good job of it. What's the matter with that, you might ask. It's just business. Right? Well, let me argue that competition is good for authors and good for books. I hope that enough indie authors will understand the complex issues surrounding KDP Select to prevent further erosion of the rich bookselling ecosystem we enjoy today.

Kindle Direct Publishing and CreateSpace are great tools to get your books sold in the Amazon.com store. But KDP Select is, in my opinion, bad for authors, publishers, and ultimately, readers.

Amazon Customer Reviews

It helps to get all your friends and family to review your books on Amazon, and you might also ask the favor of your newsletter recipients who may have read your book. Cultivate reviews from bloggers and others as suggested in the book reviews section above.

Goodreads

Goodreads is the largest social network for readers to discuss and recommend books. Amazon acquired the company in 2013. Other social networks for readers include Book Glutton, Bookish, Readernaut, and weRead.

Amazon Associates

Earn a commission on each sale of books or products by registering to become an Amazon Associate. When someone clicks the "Buy at Amazon" link on your website it'll credit you a few pennies for their purchase. This can add up! All my Amazon links in this book use my affiliate link. Smashwords and other vendors also offer an affiliate program. Use them!

MARKETING AND PROMOTION

So You'd Like to . . . guides

Write a "So You'd Like to …" how-to article in your niche topic. These are a lot like newspaper articles but are longer lived and consulted much more frequently. Consider a short excerpt from your non-fiction book.

Look Inside the Book

Look Inside lets people who are shopping browse your book much as they would if they found it in a brick-and-mortar bookstore. Kindle books are automatically enrolled in this program, and Look Inside appears about a week after publication. For your print book, sign up for a Look Inside the Book upload account and then submit a PDF. ♥

Self-Pub Boot Camp virtual workshop presentations that help you understand author marketing include those by Penny Sansevieri, founder of Author Marketing Experts, Ron Martinez of Aerbook and Aer.io on *Marketing Your Book in the Social Stream*, Mark Coker of Smashwords on *Using Pre-Sales to Make Your Book a Bestseller* and *How to Thrive in the Slowing Ebook* Market, Nina Amir on *How to Write a Short Book Fast to Build Platform and Make Money*, and Joel Friedlander on *How to Run a Successful Book Launch*. Find details on the Self-Pub Boot Camp virtual workshops and a complete list of resources at www.SelfPubBootCamp.com/resources.

CHAPTER EIGHT

SOCIAL MEDIA MARKETING

Ideally you'll start marketing and promoting yourself via your website and social media long before your book is available. Twitter and Facebook are popular with many authors because they're easy to use, enjoy large audiences and provide one-click connectivity to and from many other social media sites. LinkedIn, another popular social site, can help you to reach large groups of professionals in particular industries, and Pinterest and Instagram are great image-oriented social tools. Google owns Google+ and YouTube and so when you post there you enjoy better visibility in the Google search engine. You can also reach readers by participating in forums and groups focused on narrow topics. Let's review social media tasks and tips in this order:

- Grab your name
- Twitter
- Facebook
- Google+
- Images in social media
- LinkedIn
- YouTube
- Social publishing
- Forums and groups
- The social media rule of thirds
- Connecting with readers in the social stream
- Streamline your social media tasks
- Widgets

Grab your name

Your author name is your strongest brand so try to register yours on all possible sites. *Just to have them.* You don't have to start using them yet (maybe you won't use many of them at all), but at the very least create a keyword-rich profile that links to your website.

To keep track of all these usernames and passwords, I like LastPass. One of the useful features of a password management system (aside from the fact that you only ever have to remember one password from now on) like this is that you can grant access to your sites to others, such as to your webmaster, book consultant, or marketing assistant.

Twitter

Twitter is a great news commentary and sharing platform that can be used to provide up-to-the-second information on everything from a concert to a conference, a war or a sports event. Or just post fun facts, links to books and articles or anything at all as long as it fits into 140 characters or less. There are a lot of journalists on Twitter, so you have an opportunity to stand out as an expert or a person of interest to readers and reporters. Connect with and follow other Twitter users as well as sort tweets by topic or interest using hashtags.

Twitter apps

A Twitter app organizes your tweets, followers, and mentions. HootSuite is a browser-based tool, and TweetDeck is a desktop and mobile application. These tools also let you schedule your tweets and automatically shorten URLs, so they don't take up much space in your 140-character limit.

Hashtags

Learn about hashtags (the # symbol) so that you can communicate with interest groups on Twitter. When you start to "get" hashtags, you'll find it an incredible publicity tool. In short, hashtags are used to categorize tweets by keyword. That way you can have a conversation or get information organized by topic. Clicking on a hashtagged word shows you all the tweets marked with that keyword. Sometimes they can become what's called a trending topic. To start your Twitterverse training, find a trending topic and contribute to the conversation.

Sometimes the conversation is random and disorganized, other times an organizer sets a theme and a date and time for a group chat so that everyone can converse in realtime. You can just start a hashtag and make it happen.

One popular hashtag is #FF—Follow Friday—where a lot of people on Twitter recommend friends to follow. Here's one of my #FF tweets:

> *@missadventuring: #FF My adventurous motorcycle gal pals @advgoddess @fuzzygalore @overlandexpo @trilliumliz @madsocial @ruggedrider @daiquiric*

Facebook

Facebook separates personal pages from groups, business and author pages, virtual events, book pages, and other kinds of pages. If you're starting from scratch you'll need to create a personal page first, then an author page. (These pages are linked so that Facebook knows who owns what pages.) Use your Facebook author page to post updates on your writing, alert followers to sales, freebies, interviews and articles, solicit beta readers, and run contests. The Facebook Notes area is a great place to share stories.

Facebook also makes it easy to embed a button to place on your website so that your readers can "like" your page and see your posts in their Facebook newsfeed.

Google+

Google+ has emerged as a very popular place for writers because it displays long posts very nicely. Because of that, G+ can be used as a blogging platform. (Still, I wouldn't recommend replacing your blog with a series of G+ posts. Instead, create a short post with a teaser to your new blog post.) Once you add someone to a circle, you can target your posts to show up only on the news feeds of that circle. You can also connect with your readers, teach classes or just chat in Google Hangouts. Last summer I guided about a dozen authors through Self-Pub Boot Camp using G+ Hangouts. It was surprisingly reliable. However, Google has announced that it may not be supporting G+ in the long term, so don't invest all of your social media efforts on the platform. (Actually, this is true for any platform, which is why you need to drive people to your email newsletter.)

Images in social media

Visual content gets great results with readers. Studies show that you'll get 80% more engagement on a post that includes an image in Facebook and over 50% more clicks on Twitter. So use images to create interest in your posts and also consider incorporating visual elements like infographics or even just inspirational quotes.

Pinterest is a virtual bulletin board that lets you share links by "pinning" an image to one of your boards. Tumblr is a hosted blog tool for visual content. Instagram is a mobile app that lets you post on various social media sites. Flickr is a place to share your photos. There are lots more.

Your mobile device with a built-in camera is your best friend for keeping in real time contact with your friends, family and readers using images. Make sure to add images and infographics on your web pages so that people can share them easily using one of the Pinterest browser extensions.

LinkedIn

LinkedIn is an important platform used to reach influencers, so your profile should be as well written as a resume. Groups in LinkedIn can be very profitable places for you to spend your time. Every group has a discussions tab where you can start or contribute to a conversation. Use the promotions tab to post information about your seminars, book press releases, awards and information about articles you have written.

YouTube

Many people use YouTube to search for video content much like they use retail sites to search for products. Videos, especially a short, concise, entertaining, and well-made video, is a really good marketing tool.

Social publishing

Then, there's what's called "social publishing" used to share and discuss stories with a community of other readers. Social publishing sites help attract beta readers, writing group members and discover your markets. When you pre-publish stories or even entire books you get valuable feedback on your writing before you publish.

Two popular social publishing sites are Wattpad and Scribd, but there are many fan fiction, romance, and niche publishing sites, too. You can also publish "socially" using online stores like Gumroad, Selz, and Leanpub, which have incorporated social media features. All these sites make it easy to notify readers about your stories, books, and updates. I also like Facebook Notes for publishing to friends only.

Forums and groups

Forums and groups are great places to get attention because they're so focused and interactive. People who want to learn or to be inspired flock to them. You can become a star by sharing what you know, especially if you're an expert, as long as you don't step on the group leader's authority. You can test ideas for blog entries, articles, publicity, and invite people to friend you on Facebook and follow you on Twitter. LinkedIn is a great place for professional groups. Yahoo and Google both host groups. Meetup is the hottest group going today, perhaps because it's focused on real-world meetings. You might even create your own group.

The social media rule of thirds

The social media rule of thirds is simply this: One-third of the time you promote your book or business, another third goes to supporting like-minded authors or businesses, and another third of the time you want to just be yourself, posting things unrelated to your business but related to you as an individual.

For example, I'm an expert in a very narrow niche—women's adventure motorcycling. I give lots of advice and encouragement to other women who want to motorcycle (and to the men who love us!). But I also share my interests in publishing, gardening, yoga, travel, and my family.

It turns out that a lot of people who share those interests also like travel and motorcycling or know someone who does. They have helped me sell books, connected me with editors who pay me to write articles, and they've even helped me secure highly-paid speaking engagements at conferences, which is one of the most profitable places I've found to sell books. Best yet is the number of people I've met who live around the world and have become my friends.

Connecting with readers in the social stream

It used to be that people had to navigate to a website to obtain information but today most of us hang out in one or a few favorite social streams, collecting and passing on information to friends and trusted connections. Readers who hear about your book from their connections are more likely to follow through and investigate. You can reach them there in a number of ways.

I especially admire Aerbook's ability to drive potential buyers to your retailers. With their Flyer product, readers can preview your pages within any social stream or app. They can get downloadable samples of your book in exchange for their email address (your most valuable asset). You can also gauge the effectiveness of your program with usage metrics. Aerbook Flyer offers many more features, or you can choose from two more products, Aerbook Retail and Aerbook Plus.

Social sites for readers and authors include Scribd, Wattpad, and Goodreads, all of which have social sharing features so that site members can recommend and discuss books. In fact, lots of websites and social sites offer social media share buttons. You should include the ability to share content on your website and blog. There are many plugins that do this for WordPress users.

Streamline your social media tasks

Make your social media properties work for each other. Set them up so they automatically send updates to your various other sites. Send your tweets to your Facebook wall. Send Scribd scribbles to both your Facebook wall and your Twitter feed. If you use Goodreads, connect it, too. Search the web for how to connect one property with another. Some people find this a great time saver, others feel that each web property deserves its own treatment. You decide.

Sign up for FriendFeed to help you aggregate your feeds all in one place so that readers can get your posts delivered in a stream if they like.

One of my favorite tools is Bitly, which not only shortens URLs so you can easily paste them into your tweets without taking up the entire 140 characters they allow, but provides analytics. And that's not all. They also provide a toolbar extension that lets you share content on a web page you're visiting to your Facebook and Twitter accounts with one click.

Social media sites make it very easy to connect with share buttons. They give the ability to log into their sites using your Facebook and Twitter credentials, too. Many also provide widgets so you can display content from those sites directly on your website.

A note of caution: Be aware that, once you give an application permission to track your web activities, it might post your activities to your friends and followers. For example, SoundCloud and YouTube may post that you favorited a particular audio track or video. To prevent this from happening, turn off the auto sharing, or remember to use the "private" or "incognito" capabilities of your browser when you don't want to share.

Use a tool like TweetDeck, HootSuite, or Bitly to send updates to several networks at once. Use Feedly to aggregate all your blog and social media updates.

Create a gravatar and include your author photo and bio so that when you comment on stories on the web, you can be automatically identified.

Widgets encourage sharing

Each time you join a community, look for their "share" function or widget and consider placing it on your website. Widgets are really handy tools to display your content and social media activities directly on your web pages.

Most of us are familiar with Facebook "like" and "share" widgets and Twitter feed and "retweet" widgets on web pages these days. WattPad's widget shows off your stories and readers there. Scribd has an awesome document sharing widget that you and your fans can plug into your websites and blog posts.

However exciting all this widget action is, you'll need to decide if widgets enhance or detract from your marketing efforts at the time. If you have a new book out, maybe you don't want people clicking off to your social media sites. In that case, you'd want to remove the widgets in order to funnel readers to the book sales pages. If you want to attract people to join your social networks, then widgets can help a lot! ♥

SOCIAL MEDIA MARKETING

Self-Pub Boot Camp virtual workshop presentations that help you with social media include those by Brian Felsen, founder of BookBaby on *Social Media Essentials;* Penny Sansevieri, founder of Author Marketing Experts, and Ron Martinez of Aerbook and Aer.io on *Marketing Your Book in the Social Stream.* Find details on the Self-Pub Boot Camp virtual workshops and a complete list of resources at www.SelfPubBootCamp.com/resources.

CHAPTER NINE

EDITING & PROOFREADING

Along with everything else like marketing and social media and life in general you may be trying to finish writing, editing and proofreading your book under a deadline. Good editing, along with good design, will help you compete alongside traditionally published titles. Like every author, I struggled with editing this book and, dang it, I know there are typos because there are always typos except maybe if you're published in the New Yorker magazine, (which is famous for not having any typos).

Proofreading is the last tedious step and it seems like no matter how many people proof your book, something always slips through. About .05% of the 10,000 people who downloaded the preview edition of the book in the first week of its release found a bunch of tiny errors that slipped through and emailed me to let me know. I am so grateful. This is a big benefit of offering previews and beta editions. So this edition should be error free. (One can hope!)

Today, your book files can be easily replaced. If you find errors, make the corrections, replace your MOBI, EPUB, and the PDF for the POD print edition, too. You don't need a new ISBN as long as you have not significantly changed your book.

Developmental editing can be very expensive and this is where writing groups can be a big help. I like Victoria Hudson's *No Red Pen: Writers, Writing Groups & Critique*, intended for writers looking for information on what to consider when forming or joining a writers' group and for writers seeking tools for critiquing work in progress.

If you have the budget, a book coach or a book doctor can help you a lot. There are many of them at varying price points. Sometimes an editor can be your book doctor. Or you may need a ghostwriter. Do your research, get recommendations, and make sure you're compatible before you commit.

Instead, or first, you might look for an iterative publishing tool like Leanpub or a social publishing site (like Scribd or Wattpad) to ask for feedback from beta readers. You'll need to commit to the time and energy it takes to create a community around your book, which is never a bad idea because, in effect, this is a pre-marketing exercise.

For editing, design, and even marketing assistance you could strive to attract a publishing partner. Examples are Inkshares, She Writes Press, and Turning Stone Press. Also, as mentioned in the chapter on publishing paths, check out hybrid literary agency Fuse Literary and, if your book doesn't fit their catalog, strive to find an agency that represents your kind of book.

Remember that whenever you approach a potential publishing partner, such as an agent or small press, you should be ready with a business plan or book proposal and also make sure your title is compatible with their catalog.

Got budget? Hire it all out to a service. Examples are Authority Publishing, Aloha Publishing, Girl Friday Productions, Sellbox, and eFrog Press. These book production pros are just a few examples of the kinds of folks who can help you create a great book. I list these kinds of resources and recommendations as I learn of them, so please subscribe to my email newsletter. (And I'd love to hear your recommendations!)

Just need editing? Look for qualified professionals in your network of authors and publishers. If you belong to the IBPA you'll find recommendations there. You might also try editorial organizations, for example, the Editorial Freelancers Association and the Bay Area Editors Forum. There are more, and look for the organizations in your region, especially if you prefer face-to-face meetings. Again, I list these resources as I find them in my e-mail newsletters.

If you can't find someone by referral, there has been a boom in sites that curate book pros, including BiblioCrunch, Writerly, Booktrope, and Reedsy (based in the UK). They all pre-approve the capabilities of book professionals that join their sites, such as formatting and conversion professionals, editors, designers, author assistants, and even marketers. You still need to do your due diligence of checking references and making sure you are compatible. The editor-writer relationship is a very personal one.

To recap, there's developmental editing, copy editing (also called line editing), and proofreading. And proofreading again. It's a rare author who sets down perfect, publishable prose.

So, there are some ideas for you. Now let's dive deeper and tackle the topic in this order:

- Book consultants
- Writing groups
- Calculating time to completion
- Professional editing
- Printing proofs

Book consultants

Some people hire a book coach or production assistant at the very beginning of their project to make sure that the project is viable and that they will be able to bring it to fruition. If you don't have the luxury of a budget for this task, an effective writing group can help. Heck, hire a book coach *and* enjoy all the benefits of a writing group!

Writing groups

Writing groups come in all flavors, so select yours carefully. To state the obvious, if you are writing a business book you're not likely to obtain constructive feedback from a group of romance writers. Your writing group should consist of people who are as committed to their projects as you are to yours. They should be able to give you constructive suggestions delivered in a positive tone.

I'm lucky to have lived in areas with high concentrations of professional writers. I've belonged to three writing groups whose members were either friends to begin with or became friends after the group started. The first group was a mix of serious fiction and nonfiction writers in Santa Cruz, California. We met for a weekly *al fresco* lunch, as the weather mostly permitted, and read to each other in a leisurely fashion, and sometimes swapped printed stories.

The second group was a high-powered group of a dozen professional women travel writers in San Francisco who provided great feedback and connections with editors and publishers. Five to eight of us were generally present for a monthly meeting, hosted at one of our homes with a lavish dinner and, I must admit, rather too much wine. We handed out printed stories and read them aloud. We also worked on each others' book proposals and query letters. We produced a multimedia ebook about a trip to Ireland and self-published an anthology titled *Wild Writing Women: Stories of World Travel*, to great acclaim. Unfortunately the group voted (7 to 5) to sign it over to a New York publishing house, where it languishes today.

The third group I belonged to was the most effective in actually completing a book, as our stated goal was to motivate each other, to provide developmental editing, and finish our books, all within an intense three month period. We met every Tuesday evening at a bright, noisy Indian restaurant on Haight Street in San Francisco and spread out our papers on a large, linoleum table, taking advantage of the bottomless chai. Two of us actually did finish books, and the third member "almost" finished. My book, *American Borders*, went straight to the copy editor after our last meeting, then to the proofreader. and then I published it.

How do you know if you're in the right writing group? After a meeting, you should be energized and excited about your book. If you leave depressed and irritated, let that be the last meeting you attend.

How do you find a writing group? Search the web, post a notice on Craigslist or Meetup. Query local writing and publishing organizations and post notices at your library and local bookstores. If you live in a remote area you may form a virtual writing group. Google Hangouts is a great tool for virtual "in person" meetings.

Decide what level of critique is appropriate in the group. You might just want encouragement, or freewriting in company, or a deadline. You might, like me, want the straight, unvarnished truth. I started writing for technology in the 80s, and have formed a pretty tough shell! I have known a writer or two to dissolve in tears in critique groups, even when valid and delivered with kindness. This type of author needs to join a group for encouragement, not critique.

Calculate time to completion

There were only three of us in my last writing group. All of us were pro editors with nonfiction book projects who'd worked together in hi-tech. We made a commitment to finish our books in three months. We calculated that if we gave each other 50 pages a week we'd be done in eight weeks, and the following four weeks could be spent in editing and putting together the final draft. It really worked!

My Wild Writing Women group was awesome but not of much use when it came to book deadlines, as a monthly meeting wasn't frequent enough. We also did a lot of socializing and networking. But it was wonderful for feedback on short works like travel articles and for referrals to magazines, editors, and other publishing pros.

If you're one of those writers who work best on deadline, make up your own. Calculate the time it should take to finish your book and create a set of milestones. Schedule reminders on your mobile device and other calendars. Look at your book chapter outline and set a regular writing schedule to complete each one. Figure out how long it takes you to write the first draft of a chapter. If you keep a steady pace, you should be able to calculate how much time it will take to complete.

You might also commit to publishing your book publicly on a schedule so that your fans, even if it's just your family and friends on Facebook, can hold you to a deadline. Facebook Notes is actually great little publishing tool. Blog your book, or publish with Leanpub. You might also join a site like WattPad or Scribd to cultivate beta readers who will encourage you (and vice-versa) and perhaps even edit your work. The nice thing about LeanPub is that you can publish and even sell early versions of your work, and promise your readers updates. This makes it something of a crowdfunding platform, too.

Professional editing and proofreading

Professional editing makes a huge difference to your success in the general marketplace. A developmental editor makes sure the content is appropriate for your genre and readership, that the book has a narrative arc, that your chapters flow, and whether text needs to be moved or cut. Have you dropped a character or story line that leaves the reader hanging (or yawning)?

In fiction and creative non-fiction the plot, pace, dialog, and character development will be examined. In non-fiction, the editor will also analyze the effectiveness of lists, graphics, and illustrations. In photography and art books, a visual storyline will be analyzed.

The next step is line editing, also called copy editing. The editor makes a meticulous line edit to correct grammar, spelling, and punctuation, and consistency issues such as character speech patterns. Your editor will collaborate with you to create a style sheet.

Finally, proofreading is done once a "proof" copy of the book is printed. (See the chapter on print books for instructions on how to print proofs. I like CreateSpace.) Editing and proofreading are, unfortunately, skipped by many self-published authors, which almost guarantees failure.

To find the right editor, get recommendations from other writers. Ask for a quote. Start with one chapter to see if you are compatible or pay for a manuscript review before committing. Consider recruiting peers to do a peer review of your book. They may also become future reviewers from whom you can collect blurbs.

I also recommend a book titled *The Editor's Eye,* by Stacy Ennis, which was specifically written to take you through the often confusing process of the writer-editor relationship. Ennis rightly points out that "editors can be your very best advocates in helping you close the gap between 'draft' and 'ready for publication.'" So if you find that your enthusiasm for your book is flagging, find a good editor to work with you, and re-energize!

One more thing. I was recently amazed at the online spelling, punctuation, and grammar checking tool Grammarly's ability to find, well, spelling, punctuation, and grammatical errors. Spelling and punctuation checking is free but for grammar-checking (and plagiarism) you'll pay a monthly or an annual fee. A browser extension turns the service on for any web page you're writing on. This book was produced in PressBooks, and Grammarly automatically checked it when I opened the file for each chapter. It does the same for Facebook and other programs. Awesome!

Printing proofs

POD services like CreateSpace, IngramSpark, BookBaby, and Blurb let you order one copy at a time. Using these services to proof your text, pagination, and design is a convenient and inexpensive way to print proofs. Once your book is perfect, you can fine-tune it for printing elsewhere if you wish. I find that CreateSpace has the best prices but IngramSpark is competitive, so if you're using IngramSpark to distribute, use them to print proofs, too.

When I use CreateSpace just for proofs, I don't waste one of my ISNBs but use one of theirs, since the book will never actually be published there anyway.

IMPORTANT: Leave the publication date blank so that it's not offered for distribution.

POD services also afford you the advantage of printing Advance Reader Copies (ARCs)—with a notice that there may be errors, of course)—to send to reviewers. For more on ARCs see the chapter on print books. ♥

Self-Pub Boot Camp presentations that inform you about editing and beta reading include my talk on *Your Publishing Path* and Jessica Jalsevac's presentation on *Gumroad's Digital Sales and Distribution Platform*. Find details on the Self-Pub Boot Camp virtual workshops and a complete list of resources at www.SelfPubBootCamp.com/resources.

CHAPTER TEN

BOOK DESIGN

In this chapter, you'll learn about both interior and cover design for ebooks and print books. Interior and cover design are such different skill sets that designers specialize in one or the other, rarely both. I'll say right up front that you don't have to bother with interior design much these days because there are so many great templates available. Joel Friedlander has a bunch of beautiful, low-cost templates in Microsoft Word and Adobe InDesign to choose from. This version of the book was created in the Spark 2Way theme. You can even tinker with your template using the styles and formatting capabilities of those programs. I also recommend the free templates or themes available with PressBooks, a cloud-based book publishing platform. Blurb also provides some pretty awesome templates; they've prided themselves on great design from the start. (Visit the SelfPubBootCamp.com Resources page for links to these sites and templates.)

I'm very happy that these templates were developed because interior design is fairly tedious and really not at all intuitive to most people. There are a lot of ways that good interior designers make sure that readers love the reading experience. They tinker with fonts, leading and ligature (yeah, what's that?) to ease the reader's journey through the story in a relaxing manner, without undue eyestrain, and in order to convey information and orient them with page numbers, captions, and chapter and section titles in as unobtrusive a way as possible. This is all unconscious on the part of the reader who may or may not enjoy the reading experience subconsciously because of fonts, spacing, and page layouts.

There are also non-intuitive aspects of cover design which is why it's important to hire an expert. It might even be your smartest marketing investment.

A great cover design will grab the customer's attention and compel them to buy. Professional book cover designers are current with the ever-changing trends in book covers. They understand that today's customer may make their decision based on the impression they get from the cover as displayed on a computer screen, in a tiny size. They know that the cover must fit in with others in the same genre yet stand out enough to be noticed. I've struggled with the cover design of this book since the workbook that preceded the 1st edition and, thank you BookBaby, I think this one rocks.

Design rules for print books do not always carry over to ebooks, which require a different mindset and skillset. Much of the information here is applicable to both print and ebooks, but look for ebook formatting and conversion in the chapter on ebooks.

Design is always extremely subjective, but readability is key. Authors of text-heavy books naturally put less emphasis on design than authors of photography or children's books, who are often more willing to pay for a professional designer.

Though plain text can be copied and pasted among many different tools, design elements and stylesheets cannot be exported. If you've meticulously created paragraph styles in Microsoft Word, they'll be lost when you paste your book into InDesign and vice versa. Automatically generated headers and footers will also be lost.

You or your designer must export your book to PDF format to print it. As long as you have a PDF file you can print it with any service. The PDF can also be offered as a digital download for reading on computers and devices.

Ebook conversion services can also easily convert PDF files to create EPUB and MOBI files.

With these basics, let's dive into specific design considerations and information that will help you do it yourself or decide if you need a professional designer and how to talk to one.

- Research books in your genre
- Standard book sizes
- Interior typography, fonts, and dingbats
- Paper stock
- Spine width
- Detailed book specification
- Print book covers
- Ebook covers
- Book design services
- The importance of styles
- Design templates
- Hiring a professional
- Creating print-ready files

Research books in your genre

Book buyers who are searching for something to read perhaps unconsciously expect the cover of your book to fit a particular style. So don't make the mistake of using a curlicue font for your non-fiction book, because it will look like a romance novel. Readers are subliminally confused by deviations from genre standards. Visit Amazon,

Goodreads, and other book sites, or visit bookstores and libraries to study book covers in your genre. Here is a checklist for you.

Book size: Take a measuring tape with you to a library or bookstore. What is the most common size in your genre? (Designing a custom, non-standard book size will raise your printing costs astronomically.)

Finish: Are the covers in your genre mostly glossy or matte? Are they laminated?

Cover art: Are most of the books using graphics, photography, or a combination of the two? How about finishes?

Cover font: Look at the typography used for book titles and subtitles. Are they serif fonts with lots of curlicues (romance novels) or sans-serif fonts (non-fiction)?

Back of book: This is your chance to attract buyers. There, they find out what the book is about, why the author is so fabulously interesting or qualified, and how many important people recommend it. Notice what is tantalizing and what is distracting, and write your copy to compete.

Paper color, weight, sustainability: Do books similar to yours use crème or white paper? 55 or 60 lb. weight? (You might ask a librarian for advice, and order samples from printers.) Ask about recycled and sustainably harvested paper.

Interior font: Text-heavy books use serif fonts (they're easier to read) with sans-serif for titles, pagination, and front matter. If you see a font you like, you might find it named on a colophon page (production notes that describe the text typography, the book's designer, software used, printing method, the printing company, and even sometimes the kind of ink, paper, pulp, bulk, and cotton content.)

Dingbats and graphics: How are they being used? As chapter separators? Liberally? Judiciously? Do they enhance or detract?

Create a design folder on your computer desktop. Use Google's image search or visit Amazon to find book covers and interiors you like, and save them in a folder on your computer to refer to when you are ready to design your book.

Standard book sizes

For print books, you'll need to choose an industry-standard book size. For example, for trade paperback, choose 5.5" x 8.5" trim size (book size). The size of the InDesign the document would, in that case, be 5.75" x 9". Of course if you're using a book design template you won't have to worry about this.

Interior typography, fonts, and dingbats

Standard ebook fonts are limited but for fixed-layout ebooks and print books you have literally thousands of typefaces to choose from. A good rule is to choose one serif font (for text) and one sans-serif font (for headings, footers, captions, etc.) That may seem boring, but if you use a "pro" font you will have many more versions of the type at your disposal than just italic and bold. If your book is heavy on photography or art, you may choose to treat typography as an artistic element or choose one simple font to avoid distracting the reader from the visual story. In every case, your book's typeface will deeply, yet subconsciously, affect the reader.

You can use typographical flourishes, ornaments or characters to provide graphic elements for separating chapter numbers from chapter titles and other uses. Make sure they enhance, and not detract from, the content.

Paper stock

If you are printing your book with an offset printer, you'll have the luxury of choosing your paper stock. CreateSpace gives you a choice of white or cream. IngramSpark gives you a wider selection of paper weights.

When you start to research offset printing companies you'll learn that the elements of book design, production, and printing choices are inextricably intertwined. See the chapter on print books to understand all the issues.

You can order sample books from printers and compare the following:

- Book interior paper weight
- Book cover paper weight
- PPI
- Binding
- Cost for page count

Spine width

Getting the spine width right for each printer is tedious but must be done. Book binding, cover finish and paper weight all determine the width of the spine.

The more detail you have on your book spine the harder it will be to align correctly when you print. Some companies, CreateSpace, for example, have wider tolerances than others, which is a nice way of saying that they are not very precise with their printing. So if your spine is a different color than the front and back cover it might overlap onto the front or back. This is a good argument for using the same color for the entire front and back cover.

I always recommend using CreateSpace to experiment with your design, even if you're not going to use them to distribute your book to Amazon. They have the best prices for POD, but IngramSpark is closing the gap. So if you're using IngramSpark to distribute your book, don't bother with CreateSpace. Why a print proof? Because your book almost always looks different than you think it will and it's a great way to proofread your book, print advance reader copies, and review copies, too.

Detailed book specification

A book specification provides details for your book designer and offset printer and print broker. Choices are dictated by the size of your book and the printer's specification. Here is the information your offset printer will need, with sample information filled in. Here's some sample data:

- Quantity: 1,000; 2,500; and 5,000
- Number of Pages: 240
- Trim Size: 5.5 x 8.5
- Interior Copy: Black
- Illustrations: 24 grayscale
- Bleeds: Full (on cover)
- Paper: 100% recycled 50 lb. crème
- Ink: All black, soy
- Proofs: PDF
- Color Cover: four-color

- Binding: Perfect
- Lamination: Matte varnish full coverage
- Shrink Wrapping in 6's
- Delivery: Mac InDesign CS5 working files + laser proofs
- Shipping: address of location (residence or business)

Print book covers

Start collecting ideas for your book cover as soon as you can. You might want to collect ideas into a folder on your computer, so when you're ready to hire a designer you have something to convey. Here are the cover elements you need for the front, back, and spine of your print book. It's probably a bigger list than you expected.

FRONT OF BOOK

- Title and Subtitle
- Author (don't use the word "by" with the author name)
- Background color
- Graphics
- Photography
- Fonts

BACK OF BOOK

- Author bio
- Marketing copy
- Testimonials

- Background color
- Graphics
- Photography
- Fonts
- Publisher name
- ISBN
- Barcode and price
- BISAC standard subject headings

SPINE

- Author name
- Book title
- Publisher name
- Publisher logo
- Fonts
- Color

Ebook covers

Apple wants their ebook cover images to be at least 1,400 pixels wide. Amazon wants them 2500 pixels tall with the height 1.6 times greater than the width. B&N Nook requires a minimum height of between 1,200 to 2,000 pixels, and so on. Instead of worrying about the particular specs of each retailer I look to Mark Coker of Smashwords to set a standard that fits everyone's needs, since they distribute so widely.

Mark figures that "good-looking covers have heights that are around 1.3 to 1.65 times greater than the width." Specifically, he recommends a "vertical rectangle of approximately 1600 pixels wide and 2400 pixels tall."

He also advises that covers that are mostly text and sharp lines are best saved in PNG format. Covers that contain photographs are often too large when saved in PNG and so they will need to be saved in JPEG (JPG) format. Make sure that you use a high-quality setting, he says, so that the text doesn't come out fuzzy.

For more details and advice see this Smashwords blog post on the topic (from 2012 but still current). Find a list of low-cost designers on Mark's List of designers, formatters, and editors.

Book design services

As mentioned at the beginning of this chapter, you may not need an interior designer because there are so many great templates available. But even if you use a template you will need to apply the styles to each chapter head, paragraph, bulleted list, etc. In my opinion, every author should learn styles, it's an important part of your skillset, very easy to learn and saves a huge amount of time.

The importance of styles

Styles should be applied to each and every line in your book—chapter heads, headings and subheadings, paragraphs, headers and footers, titles, subtitles, and more. This allows you to do things like change all the title fonts from Times New Roman 18 to Myriad Pro 16, by simply changing the style. Or perhaps you want to change the body text from Georgia to Adobe Jensen Pro. One change to the style automatically makes the change to the entire book. Honestly, you are going to slap yourself in the head when you see how easy and useful it is.

In addition, you can do things like set your chapter head style to create a page break before it, and even set it to start on the next odd page. You can create sections that include the chapter number automatically in the footer, next to the page number. You can generate an automatic table of contents, too.

When I'm helping someone format their book I find it easiest to "Select All" and change everything to the standard paragraph style, then style the chapter heads and so on. You should never, ever use spaces, tabs, or returns to format a paragraph. Formatting and spacing should be embedded in the style for that paragraph.

Design templates

I just love all the design templates and themes that have been created recently. In case you haven't noticed yet, I most highly recommend Joel Friedlander's book design templates in Word and InDesign and the PressBooks themes in their cloud-based book creation tool. I've used both and can tell you firsthand how easy it is to choose a great design for export to both ebook and print book formats.

Joel also provides cover design templates, as do many others, but I'm reluctant to recommend you use them without consulting a professional. What I think works well is doing it yourself up to a point, and then hiring someone to fix it up for you. Because, as I mentioned before, it's a special skill and the cover is your best marketing tool. I know many authors, including myself, who have botched their cover designs and belatedly wished they had hired a pro.

Hiring a professional

A professional book designer is an essential marketing partner because they can help your book get noticed in a crowded market. They also know the value of typography and how to gracefully include essential elements like your logo, the publisher name, ISBN, and barcode. A professional book designer will use the latest version of Adobe InDesign.

There are a good number of designers (and formatters) on the Smashwords site who will design your ebook cover for a very reasonable fee. BookBaby and other services also provide book cover design in their suite of services. In fact, BookBaby designed the cover for this 3rd edition as well as the previous, 2nd edition.

I hope that the information in this chapter will help you to hire a good designer, and to streamline the process by being able to speak their language and prepare better by collecting assets so that you can articulate your needs.

Creating print ready files

Printing companies and print book distributors require that you upload "trouble-free PDFs" for the cover and interior of your print book. The book cover needs to include the front, back, and spine. For your ebook, you'll need to upload a JPG or a "press quality" PDF, depending on the services' requirements.

The ebook only needs a front cover but the print book needs a PDF of the front, back and spine. Each service provides instructions on how to do this.

I've been surprised at how many authors tell me they struggle with creating PDFs. Some have even bought CutePDF and other PDF conversion programs. But you don't need them. All of your applications have SAVE AS PDF or PRINT TO PDF already built in.

For example, check out Microsoft Word's instructions for creating a PDF. Do a web search for IngramSpark, CreateSpace, and others, as each vendor provides specific guidelines for PDF creation. ♥

Self-Pub Boot Camp virtual workshop presentations that help you understand book design include those by Brian Felsen, founder of BookBaby on *Social Media and Branding Essentials*, Ned Rote and Kent Hall with Blurb on *How to Make and Sell a Book*, and my presentation on *Your Publishing Path*. Find details on the Self-Pub Boot Camp virtual workshops and a complete list of resources at www.SelfPubBootCamp.com/resources.

CHAPTER ELEVEN

METADATA & DISCOVERY

Making your book discoverable to readers these days means making search engines aware of your book. Metadata is your best passive marketing partner and, as such, is one of the most important elements of your marketing strategy. After all, readers and booksellers must be able to find your book in order to buy your book. Key to this is *search*, which relies on metadata. Don't be afraid of metadata. Metadata is simply data about data or words about words.

To search engines, all words have a value and keywords have more value still. These keywords must be strategically selected and then placed where they can do the most good. Creating metadata tags is a marketing challenge that requires both editing skill and narrative common sense, two qualities that most writers possess.

People make entire careers out of SEO and metadata, but you really can do this yourself. Pay attention to how your page is ranked in search engines and look at how competing pages have gotten to the top by taking a peek at the metadata inside the metatags in their source code.

But metadata isn't the only way you get to the top of search engines. Other factors are the length of time you have owned the domain name, how active your website is, how active you are on social media sites, and the number of incoming links, to name just a few.

Metadata is used by search engines to automate a formerly labor-intensive task by connecting readers, curators, and distributors to books more efficiently than ever before. The self-publisher who understands metadata levels the playing field to compete alongside big publishing—but only if you use it. Here's what you need to know about providing metadata in all the relevant systems:

- Your keywords list
- Title and description tags
- Metadata for images
- Your Bowker record
- Metadata in documents and other media
- Metadata on reseller sites

- Metadata on social media sites
- Creating a gravatar

First, we must spill into search engine optimization (SEO) territory. The typical self-published author doesn't need to hire an SEO expert, but it helps to become familiar with the subject. Let's start with keywords.

Your keywords list

I'm going to guide you through a keywords list creation exercise. It's easy to do, and it's necessary so you can be found by search engines. Search engines and, by extension, metadata, is your most powerful marketing partner. This gets you found by readers.

You or your webmaster can insert these keywords in the appropriate places on your website, but you should also populate your bio and book description with these keywords. Here's how to start zeroing in on your keywords. (I do this in groups of three in some of my self-publishing workshops. You might want to partner with a couple of other authors to help each other out.)

Your end goal is to create a final list of no more than 10 to 20 words with a 900-character maximum, and try to keep the number of repeated keywords to a maximum of three. Use your final keywords list for your book metadata, for creating tags on blog posts, and in your social media activities.

Start by creating a worksheet to help you narrow down your keywords. I've found that most people work better by jotting ideas down on paper rather than on the computer. Get messy and cast a wide net. Then start narrowing them down. Use Google Adwords Keyword Planner to help you find effective keywords. (Detailed instructions on how to use it are provided on their website.)

Here are more tips for creating an effective keywords list.

- Record words and short phrases you think your readers might use to enter into a search engine to find you and your book.

- Eliminate the less important and more generic words and phrases from your list.

- Look at the metadata in the source code of web pages of authors with competing books to see what terms they're using. In most browsers, you can take a look at the source code using VIEW > SOURCE in the toolbar.

```
<HTML>
<HEAD>
<META name="Title" content="Carla King: Motorcycle Adventure Traveler." />
<META name ="Description" content="Carla King authors books and
travelogues about her mostly solo motorcycle adventures in America, China,
India, Africa, and Europe." />
<META name="Keywords" content="carla king, motorcycle adventure, women
adventure travel writing, motorcycle touring, american borders, china
road, indian sunset, morocco, africa, europe, moto guzzi, harley-davidson,
kawasaki, suzuki, ural, royal enfield bullet" />
<\HEAD>
<\HTML>
```

Metadata lives between the HEAD tags of the HTML in the source code of web pages.

Title and description tags

Most major search engines (like Google) no longer read keyword metatags in search results, so you must create effective TITLE and DESCRIPTION tags. (Similarly, your file names should be descriptive.)

Many website creation software programs and blog services provide you with simple forms where you can enter these various metatags, which are then inserted for you into the page's HTML source code, so it's easy to insert these tags yourself. Here are some tips to help you.

- Draft a TITLE metatag for each separate page on your website that describes that particular page, in a nutshell. Use your top keywords and make it informative first to users, and second to search engines. Set a maximum of 60 characters, including spaces.

- Finally, considering both your keywords and your TITLE, draft a succinct but keyword-rich DESCRIPTION of your book. Make this one informative to search engines first and users second. Keep it to a maximum of 150 characters, including spaces. (If you make it fewer than 140 characters, it's tweetable!)

- Also of great importance are the actual words on each web page and, more specifically, the words used in the opening paragraphs on the page, which need to indicate exactly what that page is about.

- Be sure to use keyword-rich sentences in your opening sections. For this reason, it is wise to begin each page of your website with words and not images.

Metadata for images

Metadata also includes the important ALT tags that offer short text descriptions for images. Here's what you need to tag:

- Tag the image of your book cover with ALT =["Your book title: Book description with keywords"]
- Tag your author photo with ALT =["Your name: short, keyword-rich description of the author."]
- Tag any photo on your web pages with a thorough description of the person, object, place, or other descriptive words.

You can ask your webmaster to help you do this, or, if you're using a content management system, there's probably an easy way to tag your images as you insert them into your site.

The ALT tags, like other metadata, are collected by search engines to identify and rank your pages.

Your Bowker record

Whoever buys your ISBN from Bowker controls the metadata for that book—so it should be you. Once you've

METADATA & DISCOVERY

bought your ISBNs, and your book is ready to publish, simply log in to your account on Bowker's Identifier Services page, click the ISBN number, and fill out the data in the full title detail form.

You have the opportunity to insert lots of data here—title, author, description, number of pages, size, language, copyright year, date of publication, contributors, category, title status (out-of-print, active, etc.), price, currency, book cover, and interior (to index keywords). All this information is disseminated to distributors, wholesalers, libraries and retailers (online and brick-and-mortar) so they can convey it to readers. Research the BISAC standard subject headings that describe your book category and print them on the back cover of your book next to the ISBN, and include the tags in your book and website metadata.

Keep in mind that you should be using the data here, especially your keyword-rich book description, on your website, on your marketing copy for advance reader copies (described in the chapter on creating print books) and wherever else you are advertising your book.

Here's the first page of my record for the print edition of this book. Note the "Clone this title" button at upper right. Once you've filled out the information for one format, you can clone it and change it to specify the EPUB, MOBI, and other formats. There are four pages of data, so it pays to get the first one right, so you don't have to spend time correcting each version.

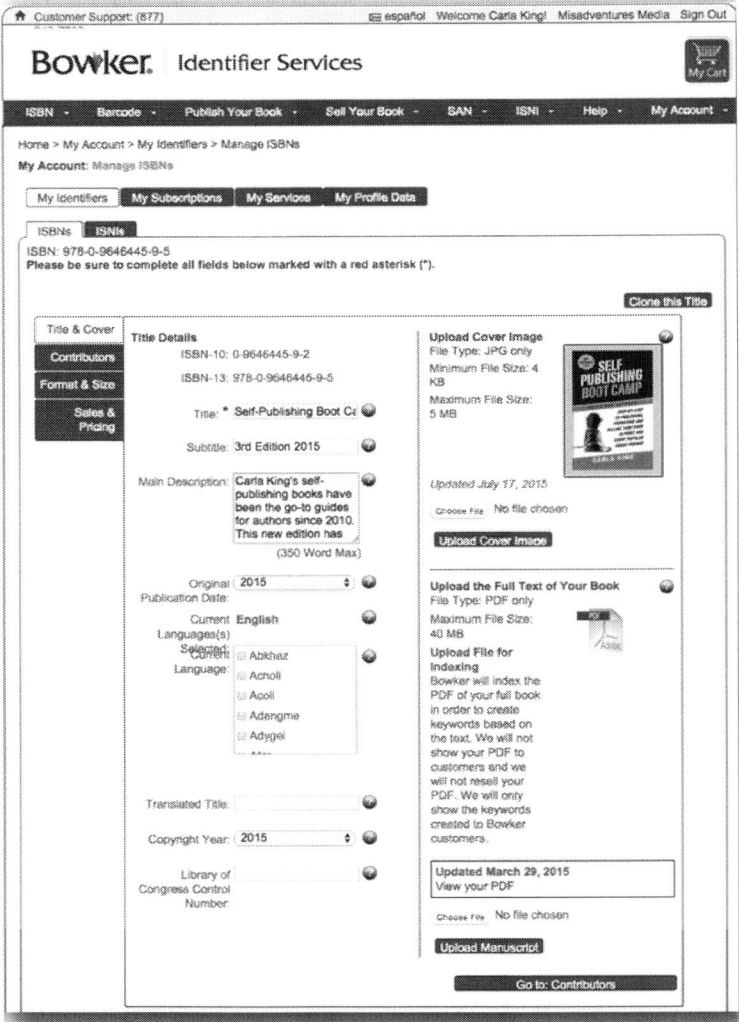

The Bowker ISBN record for this book: Self-Publishing Boot Camp Guide for Authors, 3rd Edition in print format.

Bowker also offers self-publishing services and ebook creation packages at good prices for digital books. Compare them with the digital book creation and distribution offerings from Smashwords, BookBaby, Blurb, and IngramSpark.

What is an ISBN and do you really need one?

The International Standard Book Number (ISBN) system was created to identify each published book. If your book will be sold in a retail sales channel, it needs an ISBN. Many books these days do not in fact have an ISBN, and so they're essentially off the record, making Bowker and other statistical data unreliable when it comes to the number of books published each year. So when you read something about the growth of books do remember that books without ISBNs (and there are many on Amazon) are not counted.

I have produced many books that don't have ISBNs. A multimedia travel book-like multimedia magazine to Ireland. A woman's guide to buying a first motorcycle. A guide to motorcycling Northern California wine country. These books are giveaways. I make them available in exchange for a website visitor's email address.

ISBNs consist of 13 numbers. The ISBN for the print edition of this book is:

$$978-0-9646445-9-5$$

Here's what each set of numbers represents:

Part 1: Currently either 978 or 979, identifies the EAN element (European/International Article Number).

Part 2: Identifies the country or language agency.

Part 3: The publisher identifier.

Part 4: The title or specific edition of a publication.

Part 5: The check digit.

You won't need to use these parts of numbers separately, except when you apply for a PCN, as described in the section below on how to get into libraries, you'll need to enter your publisher identifier.

Buying and managing ISBNs

To buy your ISBN visit Bowker's My Identifiers page. Buy a set of 10 or more, and also compare their ebook publishing services with others I've listed in the chapter on trusted vendors. Members of IBPA get 15% off ISBNs and all Bowker services.

Buy a block of 10 ISBN numbers. You will need to assign a different ISBN to each form of your book: print book, digital book, audiobook, and so on.

When your book is ready to publish, return to your account in myidentifiers.com and fill out all the metadata in your ISBN record so that your book will be discoverable to readers and distributors. This process is described in more detail in the chapter on metadata and discovery.

If you plan to publish more than one book, think about purchasing a SAN (Standard Address Number), a publisher identifier. The use of the SAN significantly reduces billing errors, books shipped to the wrong points, and errors in payments and returns.

You can buy a barcode from Bowker singly or in one of their packages (10 ISBNs and 2 barcodes and a QR code). Once you've assigned an ISBN and price to the barcode you cannot change it. You may not want to include the price in the barcode. Note that an ebook does not need a barcode unless you have designed it to be downloaded, printed and scanned by a store clerk. I advise waiting on this as a lot of services provide them for you. You only need a barcode for a print book, and only when you're printing it with a company who does not supply one for you. (CreateSpace and IngramSpark provide you with free barcodes, and BookBaby will sell you one inexpensively.)

A note about publishing a new edition of a book: Log in to your Bowker account and display the ISBN data for the old edition. Select, "Replaced by ISBN" and enter the ISBN number of the new edition. To take a book out of circulation, change the "Title Status" from "Active" using the drop-down menu.

What formats need separate ISBNs?

Assign one ISBN to your print book, which is uploaded to your printer and distributor in PDF format. It doesn't matter where you print it. Separate print versions (such as hardback and paperback) get separate ISBNs.

You'll need to assign an ISBN to the ebook version, no matter where you distribute. When you distribute your ebook with Smashwords, their process creates both EPUB and MOBI versions of your book (as well as doc, txt, and a bunch of other ebook formats from your single Word document). Because they only distribute the EPUB to the online retailers, record the Smashwords ISBN as an EPUB in your Bowker record at myidentifiers.com.

Because Smashwords does not distribute to Amazon, you'll need to upload your Kindle book separately. You can either use the same ISBN or none at all, as Amazon assigns a product number called an ASIN.

You can assign a third ISBN to your audio book, and a fourth ISBN could be assigned to a multimedia version of your book.

If you make small changes to your book you won't need a new ISBN. But a new edition of your book will need a new one. For example, this is the 3rd edition of this book, which means that I've now used 6 ISBNs: 2 for the first edition, 2 for the second, and 2 more for the 3rd. My book doesn't come in hardback, otherwise, I'd have needed 9 ISBNs. My pre-release version (for beta readers) did not have an ISBN.

Below is a snapshot of the Format & Size menu in the Bowker ISBN record for the print version of this book. Note that you'll be asked for details about the format by selecting from a dropdown menu. For the ebook, you'll also need to specify EPUB or Kindle. There are a gazillion other file types to choose from as well, but you're not likely to need them. For the ebook, a file size field will appear. It's important to fill out the file size field, so that retailers and customers can tell how much time it might take to download your book, and how much space on their device it will use.

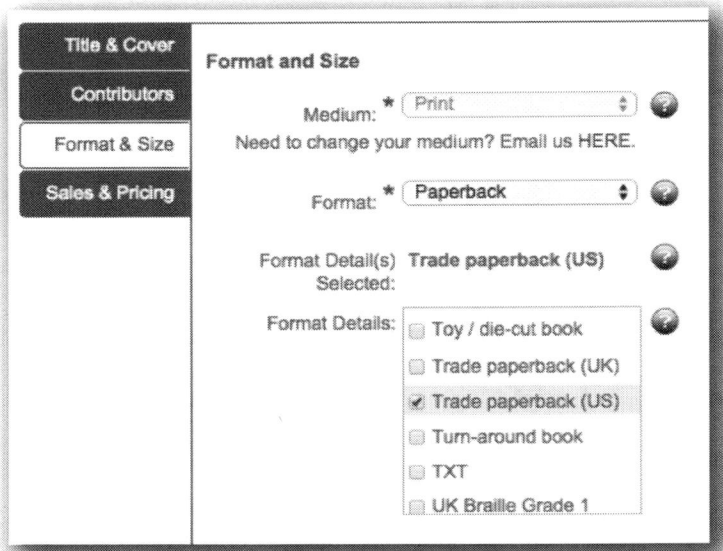

Identify your book as paperback, hardback, EPUB or Kindle in theBowker My Identifiers Format and Size page.

The medium will be either print or e-book. For e-book the format will be set as "electronic book text" but for print you'll be asked to select from a dizzying number of print format types. Just scroll down until you find the correct format.

In the Sales & Pricing menu, you'll be asked to specify who is distributing the book. If you don't see the distributor in the list, you can add yours by emailing Bowker. (There's an email link hidden under the drop down menu, below.)

METADATA & DISCOVERY

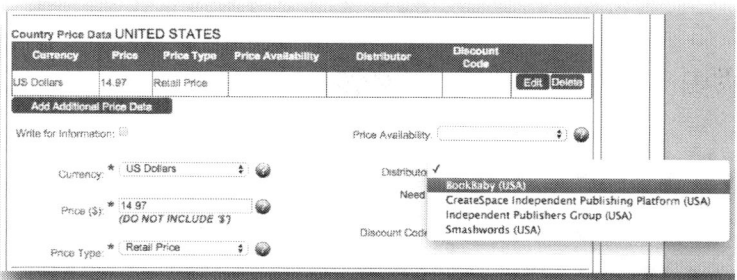

In this screen, you'll specify the price, currency and distributor for the format assigned to this particular ISBN.

Don't forget to go back and update your ISBN data once you've chosen (or changed) a distributor, know the file size, and have settled on your keyword-rich book description.

The Books In Print database

The Books In Print database supplies libraries, booksellers, publishers, and other information professionals with the details you provided about your book. Since it's managed by Bowker, your book will automatically be included in the Books in Print database. They obtain the information from your ISBN record.

Barcodes

You only need a barcode if you plan to sell in brick-and-mortar stores, where a cashier scans products with a reader. If you're selling books at events, or only through online retailers, you may decide not to buy a barcode.

Your print vendor may supply a barcode for you. CreateSpace requires a barcode and automatically plops one in the lower right of the back cover. IngramSpark includes a barcode in their cover template generator. BookBaby sells barcodes in their print packages.

You can buy an EAN barcode for your print book from Bowker or another company on an as-needed basis for your print editions. The barcode graphic must be placed in the cover art on the back of the book according to strict specifications. Follow the instructions that come with your barcode. They're quite clear on the rules for size, color, and placement of the art.

Metadata in documents and other media

Search engines take a peek inside all of the documents and applications you publish on the web for clues about their content. Almost all applications let you edit the metadata associated with the content, though they might not call it metadata. For example, metadata resides in every Microsoft Word document you create and, if it's posted on the web, search engines will collect the author and company name (yours, or the owner of your bootlegged copy) to describe it. To edit the metadata in a Word document, simply open the document and click

METADATA & DISCOVERY

FILE > PROPERTIES to change or add the data. Here's an example of what this looks like.

Metadata lives in doc files. Make sure yours has the right keywords!

If you're publishing audio, video, or any other media, make sure you edit the metadata inside that application, too. For example, Audacity, a free program handy for recording music, podcasts, and audiobooks, lets you insert ID3 tags. These tags identify the file as an audio recording to search engines and services like iTunes and Windows Media Player.

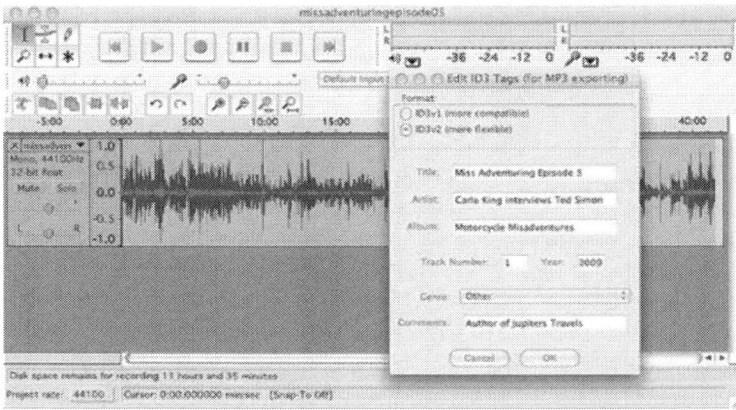

Metadata lives in audio files and all kinds of media files.

Metadata on reseller sites

Every site you publish on wants you to succeed, and so they make it easy for publishers to insert metadata. Whether you publish on Smashwords and KDP, or distribute directly to online retailers like Amazon and B&N, or upload presentations or create magazines for delivery on Scribd or SlideShare, you'll be asked to describe your document, enter keywords or search terms. When you upload your ebook as a KDP file to Amazon, you insert the same kind of metadata as for the Bowker identifier services site. Also, sign up for Amazon's "Look Inside the Book" program.

Metadata on social media sites

Never leave a social media profile field empty! Use all available information spaces on social media sites like Twitter, Facebook, Pinterest, LinkedIn, and YouTube to create incoming links to your book's web presence. Any keyword-rich author bio you can place anywhere on the web (including at the end of guest blogs and articles) is valuable real estate.

Creating a gravatar

By creating a gravatar (globally-recognized avatar) you allow your comments and activities on the web to be tracked. This helps weblogs and websites display your photo, which conveniently links to your biographical data from a central database. Register an account based on your email address, and upload an avatar to be associated with the account. This should be your author profile photo.

Some people register more than one gravatar—one for professional and one for personal use. If you're writing under a pseudonym, get a different email address to associate with that alias so that you can register a separate gravatar.

Many news and blog sites use gravatar plugins. When someone posts a comment, it checks the associated email address and displays that person's gravatar next to the comment. Your image is linked to your biographical data, which should mention your book, of course.

Gravatar also allows you to list your websites and social media activities. If you contribute to a group blog, it may also use your gravatar to identify you as the author of each post you publish.

Gravatars are critical in book promotion activities such as guest blogging and commenting on blog posts. Every incoming link to your website counts! ♥

Self-Pub Boot Camp virtual workshop presentations that help you understand metadata and discovery include those by Linda Lee on *Creating Your WordPress Blog and Website* and David Wogahn of Sellbox on *Optimizing Your Book for More Sales on Amazon*. Find out more about the virtual workshop and a complete list of resources at www.SelfPubBootCamp.com/resources.

CHAPTER TWELVE

EBOOKS

This chapter will help you to understand how to create e-books in EPUB, Kindle, PDF and other formats. I want you to have enough information to do it yourself or to hire it out to a freelancer or to choose a formatting and distribution service to do it all for you.

But first....

When most authors think about creating ebooks they think about distributing a completed ebook to all the big online retailers like Amazon, Kobo, Apple and Barnes & Noble (aka the Big 4). But I have a suggestion. Slow down and take your time to create a quality book. Edit. Design. Proofread. Avoid the embarrassment of premature publication and distribute ebooks to beta readers first. There are plenty of tools that are specially made for that purpose. (Check out my chapter on your publishing path for more information.)

You can also make money and grow your platform by sharing parts of your book or related writing. For example, you can provide a small ebook as a free giveaway when someone signs up for your email newsletter. You can grow awareness of your book by writing an article or publishing stories in an anthology. Or heck, why not create an anthology, recruiting other authors who write in your genre? So think of ebooks as marketing tools. (Find more on this in the chapter on marketing and promotion.)

Now that I've given my little speech about the dangers of premature distribution let's dive in. Here's what you'll learn about ebooks in this chapter.

- Ebook formatting and conversion basics
- Ebook formats
- Ebook readers
- Do-it-for-you services
- Doing it yourself
- Creating complex books
- Social publishing
- Ebook aggregation
- Scanning your print book
- Setting the "begin reading" point

- DRM and copyright protection
- Your digital publishing path

Ebook formatting and conversion basics

Ebook conversion is the process by which a print book is made into a digital format that can be read by ebook readers and applications. So if you have a book or manuscript you want to deliver in ebook formats, you'll need to get it converted into the various digital book formats.

First, let's define the terms formatting and conversion:

Formatting: The act of applying styles to your manuscript so that it can be read by ebook readers and apps. *You can hire someone to format your book to get it ready for conversion.*

Conversion: The act of taking the final, formatted manuscript and converting it to various formats, such as PDF, EPUB, and MOBI. To convert your properly-formatted book into the various ebook formats, you can upload it to the Smashwords meatgrinder.

You'll see the terms formatting and conversion used interchangeably, but as you see from the definitions and examples above, they are not.

To further confuse things, the term format is used in relation to styles. When you format your book, you apply styles, such as Word styles or CSS (Cascading Style Sheets) in HTML. Each paragraph in your book, like chapter heads, subtitles, body text, and bullets, needs a style assigned to it. That's another use of the word format. And then there are the book formats themselves. Let's further clarify:

Book Format: There are three basic types of book formats. PDF is the standard for print. EPUB is the ebook format for all ebooks except Amazon Kindle. MOBI is the Kindle format for delivery to the Amazon Kindle store. Wikipedia provides an exhaustive list of ebook formats, but you really only need to format your book for the most popular three. *Export your book to EPUB, MOBI, or PDF formats in one click with PressBooks. (The process of exporting "converts" the book to those formats.)*

Paragraph Format: Here, format refers to the style applied to each and every single element of your manuscript. To format your manuscript, Mark Coker of Smashwords recommends starting by selecting the entire document to apply the "Normal" style to every paragraph. Then apply the "Title" style to each chapter head. You can modify these styles to change the font, font size, and the amount of space (leading) between the paragraphs. You should never use spaces, tabs or carriage returns. *Change the style, not the individual paragraph, to create a correctly formatted manuscript.*

Paragraph Style: As in the above example, use Word styles to format a Word document. If you're using an HTML publishing tool like PressBooks, you'll also apply formats to paragraph. Under the hood, these formats are controlled by something called CSS (Cascading Style Sheets). You can apply various CSS templates to change the entire look of your manuscript at will. Styles and formats exist so that your changes can be applied globally, preventing tedious, repetitive actions to change the look of your manuscript. Every text editing program uses styles and formats, so please use them. It'll save you lots of time and money, in the long run.

Correct styles lead to correctly formatted books that can be converted into various book formats. I really hope you've been able to follow this!

Ebook formats

The major ebook formats are MOBI for Amazon's Kindle device and apps and EPUB for everybody else. These two formats will allow you to publish your book in all the online ebook retailers. There are several other formats that you may come across like Mobipocket, MSReader, and Palm, and text formats like doc, rtf, and txt. These formats are either not very widely used or are on their way out the door. You shouldn't be focused on them right now, but if your distribution service (like Smashwords) provides them, all the better.

You'll probably want to deliver your book in PDF format, too. PDF is technically for print, but lots of people use PDF for digital advance reading copies and giveaways. However, it has recently been pointed out to me that PDF manuscripts are easy to share and are pirated on sites powered by BitTorrent software. (Sign up for my email news for updates on this and other topics regarding self-publishing, copyright, and tools.)

Here's a review of EPUB, Kindle (MOBI), and PDF (print) formats.

EPUB

EPUB is to books as MP3 is to the music industry. EPUB is an open standard, meaning that no single company can control the format. Most major devices use this format. There are two types of EPUB: Reflowable and Fixed Layout.

Reflowable EPUB: Standard reflowable EPUB is great for publications where there are some images but most of the content is text. The text reflows to fit the screen of the e-reader, whether it is a large computer screen or mobile devices. Book-buyers can determine the size and even style of the font. Someone with poor eyesight can increase the font size on their e-reader, which means that the text becomes larger and easier to see. But larger text also means that there are fewer words on each page. This is why there are no page numbers on ebooks.

Fixed-Layout EPUB: The size of text on a fixed-layout EPUB book, on the other hand, does not reflow or change in size, no matter on what device it's being read. When viewed on a tablet, books in fixed-layout EPUB will look great, but they are generally too small to read on a mobile device. Fixed-layout ebooks are best for books where images tell the story.

Use fixed-layout formats for graphically-heavy books like comic books, graphic novels, graphically-heavy textbooks and children's books. You might experiment with a tool like Apple iBooks Author to reach iPad users, or Kindle Kids' Book Creator for the Kindle Fire, but generally fixed-layout books require a deeper level of expertise to create and should be handled by a professional ebook designer. Hiring someone who really understands how to make a quality fixed layout ebook will save you lots of headaches and is well worth the extra money.

Kindle

MOBI and Kindle Format 8 (KF8) are used by Amazon to deliver ebooks to Kindle devices and applications. KF8 is slowly replacing MOBI but we'll concentrate on MOBI for simple books.

Many of the same services that create EPUB books for you will also create a Kindle-formatted ebook. Or you can convert your EPUB (or HTML) formatted ebook by using a free program called KindleGen available from Amazon. It doesn't do a great job so don't make that your final book, but it's great for advance reader and review copies.

Fixed-layout for Kindle tablets are created using KF8, similar to fixed-layout EPUB as described above.

PDF

PDF is the format used to print books but people deliver docs in PDF for all kinds of reasons. It's not a great format for e-reading devices because it doesn't reflow. But PDF docs look great on computer screens and a lot of people print them out.

You might give away or sell your book or parts of your book in PDF format. Sample chapters, for example. Review copies. Personally, I like to receive review copies in EPUB or Kindle format because I don't like reading on my computer screen. It feels too much like work!

You can sell PDF versions of your books alongside the Kindle and EPUB versions. Many people sell all three formats for one price. You can sell your PDF on Scribd, Gumroad and other stores, or directly from your website.

To create a PDF simply choose SAVE AS PDF from your Microsoft Word (or other program) toolbar, or PRINT AS PDF. It's that easy!

Ebook readers

Your customers will read your ebook in on a variety of devices using a variety of ebook reading apps. E-reading devices have gone through a drastic evolution, from single-purpose devices like the Kindle and Nook to multi-purpose tablets like the iPad and Kindle Fire. People also read on their mobile devices and computer screens. More than a few of your potential customers have discovered that they can pick up where they left off on one device and continue reading on another. Personally, I do this all the time, switching from my Kindle Paperwhite to my iPhone and even sometimes, my laptop. Your book should look great on all devices, and it can.

Let me explain the technical flow. To read a book on a device, the formatted ebook must be delivered to an e-reading platform, which may not be native to the device but is delivered via an app the user can download from an app store. For example, the free Kobo app lets iPad/iPhone/iPod Touch users read Kobo books (which the publisher delivers in EPUB format). iPad owners can read Kindle books on the iPad by downloading the Kindle app.

By the way, Kindle is actually three things:

1. the Kindle ebook (document) format
2. the Kindle e-reading device
3. the Kindle platform (or app)

In the early days of ebooks, Kindle-formatted books could only be read on Amazon's Kindle reader, but then they (and everybody else) got smart and created apps so customers can read their book formats on competing devices. This means that Amazon can sell Kindle books to people who want to read them on devices other than the Kindle e-reader like the iPad, their laptop, and their mobile device.

There are many, many apps but the most popular are Kindle, Kobo, Ibis Reader (HTML5 format), EPUB Reader for Firefox, Adobe Digital Editions, and Stanza (for Apple).

The most popular e-reading devices today are the Apple suite (iPad, iPhone, iPod Touch), Amazon's Kindle and Kindle Fire, Android-powered mobile devices, any web browser (Firefox, IE, Safari), Sony eReader, Nook, and Kobo.

Do-it-for-you services

In my chapter on trusted vendors you'll find a list of companies who will not only format but distribute your EPUB and Kindle ebook to all the online retailers. Formatting a simple book shouldn't cost much more than $100 but prices can run quite high for a complex book like a cookbook in fixed-layout formats.

There are also plenty of freelance ebook pros who will be happy to be employed. The field is highly competitive these days. Subscribe to my email newsletter for a current list of my favorite vendors and independent formatters.

Get recommendations and samples from potential formatting pros. Also be clear on what devices you want to target, especially if you've written a complex books that needs to be delivered in a fixed-layout ebook format. Families of tablet computers often have different aspect ratios and so you'll need separate files for your customers who own iPads and Kindle Fires.

If you've got a complex book that needs fixed-layout formatting, you'll need to do some market research. It may be that customers who own iPads will be more likely to buy your cookbook or travel photography book. If you're selling a textbook, maybe you'll discover that most of your potential readers own a Kindle Fire.

Doing it yourself

There are lots and lots of freelancers who can format your books for you for a ridiculously low price, under $100, and it'll look fabulous on all the ebook readers. It's easy for these people, and quick, because it's what they specialize in doing. So instead of spending days and weeks on tedious formatting and validating, and uploading, hire it out. You probably don't really want to deal with with converting your Word doc to HTML and the Sigil EPUB editor and Calibre and the IDPF's EPUB Validator. So there, all in one sentence, is the list of tools for you ambitious, geeky authors who really want to do it yourself.

But listen, if you've used a PressBooks or Scrivener or Leanpub or book design templates, the work is already done for you. You won't need Calibre or Sigil. You simply export your book to MOBI and EPUB, HTML, and PDF, and give it to a distributor (or deliver to customers from your own site), and concentrate on what you do best, that is, write and market your books.

If you've got text, or a doc file, I've mentioned the importance of using styles in Word and PressBooks and other book creation tools before and I will again. Apply a style (also called a format) to each and every element of your book: chapter heads, paragraphs, bullets and any other unique styles you've decided you need. But keep in mind, the simpler, the better! Your book will look a little different in the various e-reading devices and apps, so don't become too attached to the way you think you want it to look. Your readers can change fonts and sizes and even colors, in some cases, so let it go!

Mark Coker, who founded Smashwords, wrote a book on how to format your Word doc correctly. The fact that the topic warrants an entire book might clue you in to you how complex the process can be. So this is my recommendation. If you're a do-it-yourselfer and you're using Word, just buy one of Joel Friedlander's book design templates. Then upload your manuscript to Smashwords and Amazon KDP for complete ebook distribution to the ebook retailers. Or export the Word document to EPUB, and then upload it to IngramSpark. (You could upload your ebook to the retailers on an individual basis, but that's also tedious and time consuming and, in my opinion, not worth the cost.) You can also give the Word document, EPUB, PDF, or any other type of file, to BookBaby or Bowker and let them do it for you.

If you're comfortable with WordPress (it's not difficult), use the PressBooks cloud-based publishing system to create and export your book to ebook formats. You can then upload it to the ebook distribution services, to individual retailers, or simply sell it from your own site.

If you have a full color, complex book, you're going to pay a lot to a freelancer to create fixed-layout EPUB and Kindle Fire 8 (KF8) files for you. I say "a lot" because I don't know how complicated your book is. It could be $500 worth of complicated or $3000 worth of complicated.

An alternative to hiring out fixed-layout formatting is to use Blurb, whose easy-to-use proprietary BookWright tool builds fixed-layout books concurrently with your print book (PDF) file. (They also offer InDesign and LightRoom plugins.) When you use Blurb's tools you are locked into their print and distribution services. This is not a terrible thing because it's cost-effective and they offer great quality and service, though it's priced higher than others.

If you feel completely overwhelmed by the thought of doing it yourself, or just don't want to spend the time, you can either hire a freelancer or a conversion company to do it for you (check out Mark's List on Smashwords) or use a service like BookBaby or Bowker to take control of the entire project. BookBaby, like Blurb and IngramSpark, also distributes your print book, and they do everything for you and have great customer support, as in somebody actually answers the phone. Generally, this is true for for most of the for-pay services I recommend.

If you want to give away or sell your ebooks from your own site or in other stores (PayPal, eJunkie, Gumroad, Selz, Leanpub) you can do that too, without committing to big distribution yet.

So now you see how many choices you have. Overwhelmed? Okay, here's how to streamline the process. have. For Word users, grab one of Joel's templates. For WordPress users, use PressBooks. Export your EPUB and MOBI files and give them away to beta readers, or sell them on your site. Make sure it's edited and designed beautifully. Then, when you're sure it's as awesome as it can be, then choose between 1) BookBaby, 2) Bowker, 3) IngramSpark 4) Blurb and 5) Smashwords paired with Amazon KDP. These services will deliver your ebook into all the online retailers. (Note that BookBaby, IngramSpark, and Blurb all offer complete ebook and print book distribution services.)

Creating complex ebooks

If you're a children's book author, cookbook author, or if you are authoring any kind of complex book, you have some choices to make: Kindle Kid's Book Creator, Apple's iBook Creator for iPad, Blurb, InDesign, or a combination. You could also hire a book formatting professional to do it for you.

Because the aspect ratios of the various devices differ, you need to make a marketing decision. Are your customers more likely to own a Kindle Fire tablet or an iPad? If you're writing a children's book, then try to use Kindle Kid's Book Creator. It's not yet a very sophisticated book creation tool, but it might be all you need. If it doesn't work out, it will at least serve as a mock-up for a book designer.

If you think your customer is more likely to own an iPad, then use Apple's Book Creator for iPad. You could also use Blurb. With Book Creator, you have a direct relationship with Apple, which means you make a little more money. And it also exports to PDF for print. Blurb offers a truly amazing book-building tool called BookWright with templates you can modify, and it also exports your book to PDF for print. Blurb distributes your book to Apple and can distribute your print book to a wide array of online retailers.

You can also create a fixed-layout EPUB with InDesign, the tool that professionals use. Think you want to learn how to use InDesign? Lynda.com offers a course.

Even if you end up frustrated, your work can be taken over by a professional fixed-layout book designer who will charge you at least a few hundred dollars to design your book. The superior quality can make it a more saleable book. When you have your fixed-layout EPUB in hand, you can distribute it directly to Apple or use IngramSpark or BookBaby to distribute it for you.

One more note. Because the market for fixed-layout books is limited to customers who own tablet devices, it's a much smaller market than books created in simple, reflowable EPUB and MOBI formats. So make sure your book will really only work in fixed-layout format and that there's a large enough market to make the effort worthwhile.

Social publishing

Social publishing is part publishing and part marketing. This is a chance to preview your work with your audience and ask for feedback and edits. Social publishing is a great strategy both for building readership and finessing your book for publication.

You don't need to format your book, just copy and paste your document into their interface, or upload your document to their site.

One great place for social publishing is Facebook's "Notes" feature. It's often overlooked because it's a bit hard to find. (I often resort to a google search to remember where I can post notes.) Notes is a very friendly place to start sharing because, after all, it's already populated with your friends.

Wattpad and Scribd are the two big social publishing sites but there are also genre-specific sites. For example, a lot of adventure motorcyclists share stories on ADVRider.com. Join the community, post your work and help others with their stories. You won't receive much feedback if you simply post your story and leave it there. Social publishing is a commitment.

Though not "social publishing" per se, Gumroad and Selz are online stores that allow you to offer your book for free. You can offer your book in doc, PDF, EPUB, Kindle, even audio format, and share it with your social networks.

One of my favorite tools is Leanpub, an iterative book publishing platform with a sliding scale payment option and the ability to update your readers.

No matter where it lives, you can publicize the availability of your free beta book to your newsletter subscribers and social media followers.

When your book is perfect—edited, designed, proofread and test-marketed through your social networking channels—then it's time to create EPUB and MOBI formatted ebooks to distribute to the online retailers for all the various e-reading devices and apps.

Ebook aggregation

An ebook aggregator distributes and sells ebooks to a wide range of online retailers, including Amazon (which has most of the market), Kobo (with its wide international reach), Barnes & Noble and Apple. There are many, many others.

Aggregators pay you at specified intervals and collect a percentage of revenue as their fee. Many publishers feel that the small percentage (on average, 15%), is a fair trade for centralized accounting and for eliminating the tedious process of signing up for each publishing program separately—entering your book data and your automatic payment information and uploading your ebooks again and again to obtain wide distribution.

Some aggregators also offer other services, which may include ebook formatting. (Examples are BookBaby and Bowker)

Getting your book in EPUB and MOBI for Kindle formats means your ebook can be aggregated to all the important devices and bookstores including:

- Amazon Kindle Store (Kindle devices and applications)
- Google Play (Devices that use the Android operating system)

- Sony Reader Store (Sony e-reading devices and BlueFire applications)
- B&N ebookstore (Nook devices and applications)
- Apple iBookstore (iBooks application for iPad, iPhone, iPod touch

Sales and distribution channels

A sales "channel" is a path through which you sell your book. As a self-published author you should attempt to sell your book through as many channels as you can. But understand that the law of diminishing returns is at play here and at some point the effort to place your book in a sales channel which is very small will not be worth the effort.

Here's how distribution to an ebook sales channel works. An author, publisher or aggregation service uploads an ebook file and information about your book (metadata) to the online retailer. Once your ebook is in their system, then readers can find (discover) your ebook, purchase and download it via the retailer's website or an e-reading device such as a Kindle.

If you want to hand-upload your book to each retailer yourself (though I recommend using an aggregator instead), look for the publishers' area where they spell out instructions on how to join their program. Then upload your ebook and fill out the metadata for your book, and specify how they should pay you (electronic or check).

Each retailer has a different set of rules for the amount of royalties that they will pay you on each sale. These rules can often be confusing so be sure to read the fine print carefully. If you would rather not spend the time distributing your book there are many companies who can upload your book to sales channels for you, with a centralized dashboard and payment system. (See my chapter on trusted vendors for a list.)

It is also a good idea to sell your book directly from your website using an online store. When you make sales from your website it is much easier to track where your readers came from. Here's where coupon codes really pay off, since you can advertise your book at a discount to your loyal followers.

Throughout the life of your book, continue to look for speciality websites and curators in your subject area for possible sales through their channels. For example, if you're a romance book author, create a publisher account on allromancebooks.com.

Do not cross-sell to a channel. For example, if you've already uploaded your ebook to Barnes & Noble, do not ask Smashwords to distribute it there, too. Otherwise they'll get confused and may just stop selling your book.

Scanning your print book

For those of you who already have a print book and you need it converted, where do you start? Hopefully you have a PDF file that you can hand over to a freelancer or a company that will convert it to MOBI (for Kindle) and EPUB (for everybody else).

Please don't use those free tools that say they convert PDF to EPUB for you. They do the job but your book will look awful, so you'll need to clean it up using the aforementioned Sigil or Calibre and then validate the file and *etc. ad nauseum*. You're better off using a tool that converts your PDF to a Word document, like OnlineOCR.net. It's not perfect, but at least you'll have a Word document that you can use to start formatting your manuscript.

If you do not have possession of your PDF document, you'll need to physically scan your book. The resulting document will need to be carefully proofread, because scanners aren't 100% accurate. BookBaby recommends Bound Book Scanning, a mail-in book scan service that will create a quality PDF for you, and it costs little more than $20. (And I trust BookBaby's recommendation because they have to create ebook files from this company's exports.) I'm sure there are others but I don't know enough about them to make a recommendation. If you do, I'd love to hear about them, so please contact me.

When you receive your scanned PDF, then you can ask BookBaby or Bowker or a freelancer to create an EPUB and MOBI from the EPUB. Sure, you can do it using Calibre or Sigil. But I've already given you my opinion on that!

Setting the begin reading point

When you pick up a print book, especially fiction, you're probably going to flip to the first chapter and just start reading. If you're reading a nonfiction book you're probably aiming to learn something, so you'll likely browse the table of contents to pick and choose the chapters you need or start at the introduction or even the preface.

In PressBooks, you set the "ebook start-point" in the Export Settings area of the editor. When you're formatting a book destined for Kindle and EPUB in Word, you can set the start point for the reader using Word's bookmark feature. Here are simple instructions adapted from the Amazon KDP Simplified Formatting Guide.)

In your Word doc:

> *Place the cursor where you want the book to start.*
> *Click on* **Insert > Bookmark**
> *In the Bookmark name field, type* **Start**
> *Click* **Add**

Where *should* your ebook begin? Do you want the reader to have to scroll through the cover and pages and pages of front matter? Probably not. So just in case the ebook reader or app does not start the reader off where you've correctly set the start bookmark, maybe it's best to move the bulk of the front matter to the back.

You also have an opportunity to add pages that give the reader more information about your other books and stories, and things like social media pages, invitations to beta read your next book, discounts on your products and services (if you're a nonfiction author)... anything you like.

DRM and copyright protection

DRM stands for Digital Rights Management. Every author fears copyright infringement and piracy, but please note that after a long, hard, battle the music industry no longer uses it. DRM-free books are becoming the standard, with some exceptions. EPUB for Apple will be wrapped in DRM. And the Amazon KDP format is delivered in a DRM-protected Mobipocket format. You don't have to worry about this as a separate step; the DRM is embedded in the formatting.

It is always illegal to pirate books and music, and to steal another person's writing, and instances are rarer than you think. It might be argued that undiscovered self-published authors should be happy to suddenly become widely pirated. Then you can take steps to correct it, and write a press release to let everyone know how popular you are.

> *For a typical author, obscurity is a far greater threat than piracy.* —Tim O'Reilly

You can easily and cheaply obtain copyright protection by registering your work with the copyright office as described in the chapter on doing business as an author.

Your digital publishing path

To recap, there are multiple paths to ebook distribution starting with social publishing and beta readers to help you build your platform.

You can pre-publish stories from your book or even your entire book to a social publishing site like Scribd or WattPad to get feedback from readers. Leanpub is also an excellent venue for beta readers and to make money from your unfinished book. See the section on marketing and promotion for ideas on how to cultivate a community and attract beta readers.

You might also want to create digital ARCs for reviewers privately using Smashwords or Scribd. Also, consider Gumroad and Leanpub.

Make sure you get great editing and design before you format for EPUB and Kindle readers and for distribution to the online stores.

Upload your books individually to the various online retailers, or outsource it to one of the services I mention in the chapter on trusted vendors.

Sell your ebook directly from your website using an online shopping cart or sales widget that allows you to automatically deliver digital downloads. ♥

Self-Pub Boot Camp virtual workshop presentations that help you understand how to create and distribute ebooks include those by Robin Cutler of IngramSpark on *Distributing to Online Retailers and Getting Your Book into the Bookstores,* John McAlester of PigeonLab on *Ebook Conversion, Formatting and Distribution Basics,* Ned Rote and Ken Hall of Blurb on *How to Make and Sell Books,* and Mark Coker of Smashwords on *Using Pre-Sales to Make Your Book a Bestseller.* Find details on the Self-Pub Boot Camp virtual workshops and a complete list of resources at www.SelfPubBootCamp.com/resources.

CHAPTER THIRTEEN

PRINT BOOKS

For those of us who want to print our books, there are almost too many choices. You can use a POD vendor to experiment with interior and exterior designs, as well as print galley proofs for final proofreading. Then you can print a short run of advance reading copies (ARCs) for reviewers. After you are sure the book is perfect, you may choose to continue using POD or short-run vendors to avoid holding inventory or decide to invest in a large quantity of offset print books.

Authors of full-color books who want to distribute their books on-demand (POD) have fewer options because quality color printing on demand is very expensive and the color quality is not as high as that done by offset print equipment. A good solution is to use CreateSpace to test your design first and proof your book. Or use Blurb for a high-quality proof of your color book. Then, when your book is perfectly designed and proofed, and you're sure you can sell a large print run, use a print broker to find an offset printer, often located in Asia.

If you are publishing both a print book and an ebook, you may want to look for a vendor that does both. These include BookBaby, Blurb, and IngramSpark. You may find it easiest to use one of these vendors, or you might find reasons to use a combination of vendors. For example, Smashwords and KDP for ebook distribution, CreateSpace for printing proofs and to distribute directly to the Amazon store, and BookBaby or IngramSpark to distribute your print book to all the other stores.

Here is your step-by-step guide to creating and distributing print books.

- Print your proof
- Advance reading copies (ARCs) for reviewers
- Print-on-demand (POD)
- Short run printers
- Offset printing
- Full-service vendors
- Bar codes

Print your proof

I like to use CreateSpace to experiment with book design and for final proofreading. They don't charge any upfront fees, they're easy to use and send books quickly.

Many first-time publishers print and correct many times until they feel the book is right. So test printing with a POD company is a smart strategy, especially if you're sending ARCs to reviewers to build your platform and promote your book.

Advance reading copies (ARCs)

It's traditional to send book reviewers an ARC several months in advance of publication, but these days most authors send the book out to reviewers and release the book at the same time. You can print these books using a POD service like CreateSpace, or print a short run with a service like 48HrBooks. IngramSpark and Blurb also allow you to print one copy for review. But I've found CreateSpace the least expensive and fastest.

Bloggers and other casual reviewers might review your book immediately, but if you want reviews in Foreword or other traditional channels, you'll need a four- to six-month lead time.

It's okay to send an imperfect book for review as long as it's marked "Publisher's Proof" or "Advance Reading Copy."

Here's what you need to print on the front and back cover of the book if you're sending out ARCs. (Do this even if you are only sending electronic ARCs.) I know this is the chapter on print books, but I'm including information pertinent to creating ebook ARCs as well.

Make sure the cover is prominently marked with the disclaimer ADVANCE READING COPY. It should also be marked "Publisher's uncorrected proof—not for sale." If your cover art is not final (or close enough), you can create a separate, plain, single-color cover just for the advance copy.

On the back cover, list the following information so that reviewers can reference this information in their book reviews:

- Release date
- Number of pages
- Book size
- Formats available (print, MOBI, EPUB)
- Sales channels (for example, "all the usual online retailers")
- Price (for each format)

- ISBN (for formats, sales channels - print, Kindle, and EPUB - for example, or print, Kindle and Smashwords. More on ISBNs in the chapter on metadata and discovery.)

- Author photo (see the branding chapter)

- Link to the media kit on your website (More about this in the marketing chapter.)

- Put a notice on the back of the book that reads something like the following.

> *PLEASE NOTE: This is an uncorrected proof. Any quotes for publication must be checked against the finished book. Price and publication date are subject to change without notice. Inquiries should be directed to Misadventures Media at carla@carlaking.com.*

Also include a "one-sheet" description of your book with all the above information and marketing copy. Make sure to use your keywords. This is probably the same copy that you insert in the Bowker database when you're assigning the ISBN for your book. See more about ISBNs, metadata, keywords and book descriptions in the chapter on metadata and discovery.

To use CreateSpace to print an ARC, upload the PDF of your interior and cover. The cover does not have to be designed yet. In fact, it can be a plain white wrapper with pertinent information printed on it. Use one of CreateSpace's ISBN numbers and leave the Publication Date field blank. Make sure to make the reviewer very aware that the CreateSpace ISBN is NOT the book ISBN. I suggest printing the actual ISBN on the front and back covers as well as on your one-sheet, in large type.

Print-on-demand (POD)

Printing on-demand is a low-cost and risk-free way to do business because you don't hold inventory. The downside is that it costs more per book for print-on-demand than it does to print a lot of books with an offset press (which also prints higher-quality books, though that gap is closing as the machinery improves). CreateSpace, IngramSpark, and BookBaby all provide print-on-demand books, and the latter two also print short runs and offset in quantity. For super high-quality color books printed on-demand check out Blurb.

Short run printing

Short run printing is a great option for authors who plan to sell ebooks online but who also want to create print versions of their books to sell at events. There's not a lot of difference between the cost of POD and short-run printing though, so compare prices from CreateSpace and short run services like 48 Hour Books.

Offset printing

Offset print books are of higher quality and much cheaper per book than POD printing because of the machinery and quantity—though most offset printing companies won't print fewer than 1,000 books at a time more but and more printers are dropping the quantity to 500. A print broker may be able to get you a better deal on offset printing.

Authors with full-color, photography, and children's books are most likely to want to print high-quality books with an offset print vendor, and should definitely consult a broker.

If your book is a standard trade paperback, and you know you can sell hundreds of books at a time, then it's very cost-effective to find an offset print vendor to print at least 1,000. You may sell the other 500 at events and from your website faster than you think. And don't forget the freebies you can send to important people during your promotion activities.

Offset printing can take six to eight weeks from order to delivery—more if you are printing a full-color book overseas. Don't forget to factor in the proof approval process. If you are printing a color book, you will definitely want to check that the four-color process results in the four colors you expected. So plan ahead.

Before we get into the process of creating RFQs and choosing a print broker, let's take a look at a streamlined path for authors of full-color print books.

- Design your book using a template or in InDesign, or use Blurb for the whole process from design to distribution.
- Upload a PDF to a vendor like CreateSpace or Blurb to print proofs, make corrections, and tinker with the design until the book is error-free.
- Find a print broker to hire an offset printer (often located in Asia) to print a quantity of books.
- Order a proof from the printer, to ensure that the color is perfect.
- Order the printed books.
- Distribute them from your website, using a distribution service, or on consignment with Amazon Advantage. (Blurb has an end-to-end solution.)

Create a PDF ebook version of the book that looks exactly like the print book, minus the blank pages, to sell online. Blurb's BookWright tool, however, creates your print and fixed-layout ebook concurrently.

Optionally, or in addition, get the book converted to the iPad fixed layout format, an EPUB extension that uses CSS to make the book content flow beautifully inside the iPad, and to Kindle Format 8, the EPUB-like format that can be read by the Kindle Fire tablets.

Compose a Request for Quote (RFQ)

If you sent out 100 RFQs you could get 100 different price quotes. It's much easier to enlist the help of a print broker (described in the next section) if you are printing a full-color book. Either way, you'll need the following information.

- Your name, address, and contact information: For your printer and their shipping company.

- Book specs: Size, number of pages, paper weight and color, recycled, soy ink, etc.

- The quantities you'd like quotes for (750; 1,000; 2,500; etc.).

- Cover lamination: Matte or glossy.

- Shrink wrapping: This helps keep books clean, and you can sell books in sixes or tens, too.

- Cover overruns: You want them. They're great for book displays.

- Delivery to a residence: May require delivery by small truck.

- Full bleeds on cover (probably) and interior (mostly for photography and art books).

- How you will deliver the files. For example: "PDF cover and interior created in Mac InDesign CS5."

Hire a print broker

Enlist the help of a print broker—they know the market and which printers are likely to give you the best price and the best quality. They will quote you print prices with their percentage already factored in. You may be surprised that, even with their cut, they can get lower prices than you can. That's because they have long-term relationships with printers. Also, it is not in the printer's interest to supply brokers or their clients with a poor quality product, where they may think they can get away with it with a one-time client.

Search the web to find print brokers. If you're a member of a publishing organization like IBPA, they'll have a list. Talk to as many print brokers as it takes to find one you like and who likes you and believes in your project. Ask for samples of books from the printers they represent and also for client referrals.

Full service vendors

More vendors than ever are now offering multiple printing services: POD, offset, digital short runs and ebook printing and distribution. They may also have deals with major distribution channels that serve brick-and-mortar stores as well as online and ebook marketplaces.

You only have to upload your book file once, you have one contact point, and you can concentrate on writing and promotion—the two things nobody else can do for you. Co- and partner-publishers like book packagers, distributors, printing companies, small presses, literary agents, and author services companies offer varying levels of service quality in this area. Refer to the chapter on tools and services I trust for a list of full service vendors who can do this all for you.

Barcodes

If you're printing using a POD printer you probably won't need to buy a barcode separately. IngramSpark and CreateSpace, for example, provide them for you. BookBaby provides low-cost barcodes with their service.

Only if you're printing your book with a traditional offset printer or short run printing company do you need to provide your own barcode. You can buy high quality barcodes from Bowker, who has a thorough barcode FAQ on their site.

Alternatively, you can get a free barcode from Lightning Source by using their book cover generator. The returned file includes the barcode, which you can copy and paste into your artwork. (Or hand it over to your designer to paste in.) Resist buying cheap barcodes, they actually don't work very well.

You can choose to embed the price of your book in the barcode or not. I do not include the price because I sell a lot of books at conferences and other events, and sometimes I charge more for an autographed copy. Also, taxes vary in counties and states, so it can be confusing to buyers who are asked to pay $21.95 for a book priced at $16.95. At events, I usually price my book at a flat $20. It's easy, fast and, as long as there's no price on the back, nobody complains. ♥

Self-Pub Boot Camp virtual workshop presentations that help you understand how to create and distribute print books include those by Robin Cutler of IngramSpark on *Distributing to Online Retailers and Getting Your Book into the Bookstores* and Ned Rote and Ken Hall of Blurb on *How to Make and Sell Books*. Find details on the Self-Pub Boot Camp virtual workshops and a complete list of resources at www.SelfPubBootCamp.com/resources.

RESOURCES

Whew! You got all the way to the back of the book. You didn't flip right to this section, did you? That's okay, there's plenty of time to peruse this book as you need the information. I also provide updates, tips, and resources delivered by email, along with updates to this book, online workshops, webinars, special offers, discounts and freebies from my network of self-publishing experts. Please subscribe to my writing and publishing news on SelfPubBootCamp.com.

Now, on to the list. Here are the books, organizations and classes I refer authors to most often:

Self-Pub Boot Camp and other classes: This is my virtual offering to you, bringing over a dozen experts to your desktop to help you decide how to create, publish, promote and sell your books. It goes beyond the basics to generate ideas and create enthusiasm as it makes you aware of imagination-stimulating possibilities. With audio, video, slidesets, handouts and ebooks from the presenters, all extremely well-respected self-publishing pros.

The Self-Publisher's Ultimate Resource Guide: Every Indie Author's Essential Directory—To Help You Prepare, Publish and Promote Professional Looking Books by Joel Friedlander and Betty Kelly Sargent

Time-Saving Templates: Joel Friedlander is The Book Designer, and lately he's been creating some great templates that save you time and make you look like a pro. Joel has partnered with other experts to package their expertise in a form you can download to fill in the blanks and get it done fast. I highly recommend all of these products.

- Interior Book Design Templates
- Book Cover Template
- Media Kit Template Bundle
- Blog Template Kit

How to Write a Book!: To Get More Opportunities and Improve Your Career by Andreas Ramos. If you're not sure how to proceed, this book is the bomb!

Publishing 101: A First-Time Author's Guide to Getting Published, Marketing and Promoting Your Book, and Building a Successful Career by Jane Friedman has the most practical advice on steps you can take as an author self-publisher that I've yet found.

How to Blog a Book: Write, Publish, and Promote Your Work One Post at a Time by Nina Amir. I love this book and Nina's plan to blog and create a book at the same time. Timesaving, inspiring!

How to Write a Short Book Fast: In this mini-course with Nina Amir, you will receive all the information you need to to decide what structure best suits your needs, genre, and topic. Write a short book to give away to people who sign up for your email newsletter or make money selling short, information-packed booklets at conferences and other events.

Author Training 101: How to Craft Books that Sell is a great program with Nina Amir. It provides a step-by-step process that helps you create a successful book AND to train you to succeed as an author. It does that by teaching you how to produce a professional-quality business plan for a book, otherwise known as a book proposal, evaluate your book idea for marketability (by publishing industry standards), and become the type of writer who can self-publish successfully or attract a publisher. In the process, you'll learn to craft a book that sells—and to help it sell.

Self-Publisher's Legal Handbook: The Step-by-Step Guide to the Legal Issues of Self-Publishing by Helen Sedwick

Secrets to Ebook Publishing Success by Mark Coker of Smashwords

Independent Book Publishers Association Membership includes education, marketing opportunities, community and much more.

And there's more! Please also check out my blog posts on the Self-Pub Boot Camp site, where you'll also find updates on this list and information on personal appearances and virtual workshops. There are also lots more bloggers, books and resources I want you to know about. So please subscribe to my writing and publishing news to stay up to date. ♥

ABOUT THE AUTHOR

Carla King is a travel and technology writer and founder of Self-Pub Boot Camp, a program of books, workshops and seminars. She began her self-publishing journey in 1994 with a book about bicycling the French Riviera.

In 1995, she pioneered the art of the realtime online travelogue with *American Borders,* reporting live on the internet from a journey around the edges of the USA on a cranky Russian sidecar motorcycle. She continued the series with trips in India, China and Europe, reporting back by blogging (though the term "blog" hadn't yet been coined).

Today, Carla combines her love for travel, writing, publishing, and technology by splitting her time between Self-Pub Boot Camp and her adventure travel activities. She also splits her time between Baja, on the Sea of Cortez, and San Diego, on the Pacific Coast. She is a regular presence at adventure travel and writing conferences in California and the Pacific Northwest, as well as Overland Expo and Horizons Unlimited. Her daylong intensive Self-Pub Boot Camps are recorded and offered virtually on SelfPubBootCamp.com. You can find her travel writing at CarlaKing.com ♥

ACKNOWLEDGEMENTS

I am fortunate to have grown up with the self-publishing revolution, watching in fascination as the founders of many of the products and services mentioned in this book developed and perfected their platforms. In the past ten years, we've met at conferences to trade ideas, discuss and dream about how to serve authors and the readers who want their books.

During the course of our acquaintances, I learned that most of these founders had experienced a barrier in the publishing process themselves, figured out how to solve it, then realized that everybody else needed the same solution. Maybe that's why they have been so extremely generous with their time and transparent in their business processes. I appreciate their enthusiasm, honesty and dedication to improving the lives of us indie authors. Because that is what happens. Our lives are improved because they've made it so much easier to publish, and now we can maybe even make a living from writing. Thank you.

In particular for this edition I want to thank Tom Laverty for the awesome push to the finish line by offering an early version of this book as a promotion for BookBaby, a company I've long admired. Also, much appreciation goes to Hugh McGuire of PressBooks, which is the tool I used to create, edit, and produce this book in PDF formats for print and digital delivery. I love the custom theme!

I also want to thank Dan Poynter, the self-publishing guru who assisted me and so many other aspiring self-publishers through the process that was so very daunting way back then. I turned to his manual in 1994 when self-publishing my first book. It was a great success!

Finally, I thank the many authors who have let me know that I've made a difference over these past five years with the Self-Pub Boot Camp books and workshops. I'm constantly astounded at your talent and dedication, and I have so much pride in your success. I love technology for its ability to spread knowledge and to keep in touch. So please, do keep in touch! ♥

EVENTS, WORKSHOPS & CONFERENCES

Self-Pub Boot Camp workshops are recorded and available for virtual online learning, along with supplementary materials and bonuses. Look for an evolving program of audio, video, books, and classes through the year. For more information visit SelfPubBootCamp.com ♥

WHAT NEXT?

Here are some suggestions.

Metadata first. It sounds geeky and difficult but it really isn't. Once you figure out what keywords to use, it'll be a lot easier to write your author bio and book description. Then you can start populating this information throughout the web to start the discovery process.

Put a simple Wordpress website up and use MailChimp to get your email newsletter on the site. You want to get email addresses from everyone who visits, starting now.

Get feedback on your book. Blog a bunch of it, or share it on a social publishing site. Cultivate beta readers. Join a writing group. Make your book a fantastic read.

Start collecting images and book covers that you like so that your designer can almost read your mind. It'll save a lot of time, money, and frustration. Most authors leave this to the last minute and, I can tell you, it's painful!

Build platform. Publish often! Write articles, contribute stories, blog, create a magazine, compose short books.

Connect with your writing community and keep learning. Visit selfpubbootcamp.com to sign up for my email newsletter and get lots of tips, news, and updates about what's going on in the world of self-publishing.

Thousands of authors have downloaded this book, and many of them have written to tell me that I've saved them hours, days, even weeks of time and research. That makes me happy!

REVIEW THIS BOOK

I'd really appreciate an honest review on Amazon. I strive to make each edition better than the last. Find the book on my author page by typing *Carla King Amazon Author Page* in your search engine. Or type in this URL: http://www.amazon.com/Carla-King/e/B004FWBLQ6

THANK YOU!

Made in the USA
San Bernardino, CA
11 November 2015